MOUNTAIN BIKING

MOUNTAIN BIKING

Max Glaskin and Jeremy Torr

PELHAM BOOKS

PELHAM BOOKS

Published by the Penguin Group
27 Wrights Lane, London W8 5TZ, England
Viking Penguin Inc., 40 West 23rd Street, New York, New York 10010, USA
Penguin Books Australia Ltd, Ringwood, Victoria, Australia
Penguin Books Canada Ltd, 2801 John Street, Markham, Ontario, Canada L3R 1B4
Penguin Books (NZ) Ltd, 182–190 Wairau Road, Auckland 10, New Zealand

Penguin Books Ltd, Registered Offices: Harmondsworth, Middlesex, England

First published 1988

Typeset, printed and bound in Great Britain by Butler & Tanner Ltd, Frome and London

A CIP catalogue record for this book is available from the British Library

ISBN 0 7207 1857 0

Contents

Photo Credits 6

1 *Easy Rider* – the Evolution of the Mountain Bike 7

2 Buying a Mountain Bike 16

3 How to Ride your Mountain Bike 37

4 Where to Ride your Mountain Bike 53

5 Maintaining your Mountain Bike 63

6 Recreation and Ride Planning 85

7 Competitive Mountain Biking 97

8 Urban Mountain Biking 108

9 *Moving On* – Accessories and Clothing 116

10 A Great Adventure 132

The Mountain Biking Directory 140

Index 149

Photo Credits

The authors and publisher are grateful to the following for permission to reproduce copyright photographs in this book: page 8 *Evening Standard*; pages 12, 20, 27, 51, 65, 106 Muddy Fox; pages 15, 28, 32 (above), 35, 42, 43, 46, 49, 50, 67, 69, 71, 72, 73, 74, 75, 76, 77, 82, 109, 123, 127 Mountain Bike Club; pages 25, 32 (below), 33, 34, 36 Shimano; page 121 Bluemels SKS; pages 125, 129 *Freewheel*; page 130 Richard Ballantyne; page 133 Intermediate Technology.

1 Easy Rider – The Evolution of the Mountain Bike

Mountain biking is about enjoying the tranquillity and beauty of the countryside. It is about riding a sturdy and easily-controlled bicycle, away from the traffic-laden roads. It is about exercise and enjoyment. It is about getting lost in the middle of nowhere with impassable trails in all directions, then finding your own way out of the mess. It is about having a lazy day with friends in the open air. It is about struggling up hillsides to set personal records and it is about learning skills which are the envy of trick cyclists.

A mountain bike is your own magic carpet. As long as you provide the power and the nerve it will go almost anywhere. And it is built to make the journey easy, whether on the road or off it.

There is something about a mountain bike which is instantly visually appealing. Perhaps it awakes a common folk memory of those huge old black sit-up-and-beg roadsters which were favoured by district nurses and bumbling policemen in *Carry On* movies. More likely, it is the sturdy shape, the tough style and the loud paintwork which overshadow other bicycles. Whatever makes you opt for the moon buggy of the bicycle world in preference to the milk float, once you step aboard you will be hooked.

The desire to pedal towards yonder horizon, in a straight line, ignoring all obstacles, is strong. The saddle feels comfortable. The handlebars are at the right height. The gear and brake levers are at your fingertips. The fat tyres cushion the bumps. The low gears make pedalling a doddle. Cycling was never easier.

Once at home on the bike you may be tempted to try a few things you have not done since you were nine years old – swooping down inclines, thrashing up hills, jumping imaginary logs and whizzing in a spray of water through mountain streams. Afterwards you will be as happy as a pig in a mudbath – enervated, filthy and full of the joys of mountain biking. You may have fallen once, you may have stumbled a couple of times and got off to push, but it doesn't seem to matter. Away from the road, few people will have seen your errors and anyway, you can blame the terrain for your mistakes. On the whole mountain biking is very easy, but it always tempts you to try something a little harder, a little more exciting. And when you succumb to that temptation and succeed in your attempt you will be perfectly justified in feeling pleased with yourself.

Mountain biking is a cross between skiing, cycling, botany, bird-watching and weight-training. The rewards are just as varied.

There have been mountain bikers for almost 150 years, although until the last decade they have had to do without bikes designed specially for off-road riding. When Kirkpatrick MacMillan built the very first bicycle in 1839, he struggled along the unsurfaced and pot-holed coaching roads of Scotland in much the same way that a modern mountain biker might tackle a bridleway. Unfortunately, he set a bad example (or perhaps it was that the authorities decided to make an example of him) by being the first cyclist to be successfully prosecuted for breaking the laws of the highways.

The huge popularity of cycling among the growing Victorian middle classes led to the formation of the Cyclists' Touring Club which successfully encouraged the authorities to surface roads with a smooth, weather-sealed and durable covering. The comfortable ride was further improved by two later innovations – pneumatic tyres and tarmacked roads, which sowed the seeds for cycling to be viewed as an on-road pursuit.

But primitive mountain biking continued, out of necessity. Bicycles were used by homesteaders and pioneers throughout the New World, and adventurers the world over were pedalling heavyweight diamond-framed bicycles along dusty trails and up mountain tracks. There is nothing new about mud-plugging.

In the early twentieth century the development of the motor vehicle made cycling an increasingly hazardous and unpleasant

Opposite *Ride a mountain bike and enjoy yourself.*

activity. Followers of the 'outward bound' school of thought took to riding hill tracks to get away from the traffic and to keep in touch with nature. On a rock high up in the Berwyn hills of Clwyd in North Wales, above the Ceiriog valley, which the motoring guides mistakenly call a 'cul-de-sac' valley, is a metal plaque dedicated to a cyclist known as Wayfarer. He was one such off-road enthusiast and he blazed so many trails that he became a legend among 'rough stuff' riders. He showed that where a horse could go, so could a bicycle.

Despite this long tradition of off-road cycling in Britain, which must include the post-war sport of cyclo-cross, it seems that few people considered building bikes specifically for leisure riding in the dirt. Perhaps we had become too enamoured with the tarmac ribbons which make the countryside accessible whilst necessarily scarring it. Perhaps nobody had thought it was possible to make a bike which would not break or seize up in tough conditions. More likely, the British cycle industry lacked the imagination and courage to innovate.

So we have to look to the United States for the first twinkle of mud in the cyclist's eye, whilst noting that the US is the home of the instant legend and the modern myth. Nevertheless, it seems clear that the modern mountain bike was conceived, like innumerable Californians, on a hillside in Marin County.

If you don't know Marin County then you could do no better than to read *The Serial* by Cyra McFadden. The area is revealed as one where anything goes, where the social revolution of the 1960s has evolved into an art-form. And it is where, in the Seventies, a group of freethinkers stole kids' bikes and wrecked them by going hell for leather down the sides of local mountains.

The bikes they rode were like the one ridden by Pee-Wee Herman in his film *Pee-Wee's Big Adventure*. They were the standard children's bikes before BMX came along and they had been on the go for forty years. Weighing up to 50 lb with lots of curly tubing and as much chrome as was fashionable, they had been designed to be the young rebel's ultimate roadster. They were slow to accelerate because they had just one gear, and slow to stop because they had pathetic hub brakes. But the adults claimed they were perfect for off-road, down-hill riding because of their laid-back frame design. The geometry of a bike determines how it handles and when you are touching 40 mph down a dirt track you want something which responds well. You also want something which stops when you put the brakes on and something which does not weigh 50 lb when you have to push it back to the top of the hill for another thrilling descent.

So the technically-minded of this growing band came up with improvements. The hub brakes, which had to be overhauled at the bottom of each descent, were replaced by rim brakes, and gears were added so that it became possible to pedal up gradients. New frames were built out of lighter steel alloys. All that was left of the old cruisers was the frame angles and the balloon tyres.

The mountain bike was born. It was an ugly duckling which has never grown into a swan and would not work if it did. Yet the exhilaration of hitting the trail and the adventure of pioneering new routes began to catch on. Bicycle framebuilders were receiving more and more orders for mountain bikes and eventually the mass-producers joined in. The industry was still in shock after the massive popularity followed by the swift decline of BMX. Fortunately, there were importers left who were ready to take a chance and instruct their Far East frame-suppliers to use suddenly vacant factories to produce mountain bike frames. Spare BMX components were also put to good use.

Bicycles have over 1,000 components and it became necessary to make these stronger for mountain bikes. After all, when you have been inspired to leap the Grand Canyon on your fat-tyred stallion you don't want to foul the run-up by crunching the gear mechanism. So the major Japanese manufacturers, and their gaggle of imitators, worked hard to provide stronger, more durable and more forgiving components. Bearings, gears, chainrings, stems, rims, brakes, cables and levers were redesigned almost annually to offer the dedicated mud-plugger a reliable and faithful range-rider.

All this innovation was expensive and many manufacturers were taking huge financial risks in what was an unproven market. But the customers were there and they willingly paid the initial high prices to join their peers in the Californian hills, in the Colorado mountains and in the wilderness areas throughout the US.

In 1983 the first mountain bikes appeared in the UK. There had already been a few odd-bods (one of the authors included) designing and building off-road machines but it took an American trend to provoke the home industry into supporting the activity on any scale. Half a dozen Tom Ritchey bikes were imported and *Freewheel*

The shot that launched a thousand mud-pluggers, seemingly giving mountain bikers the power to ride on water. It was taken in 1984 and launched the first large-scale bike sales campaign.

advertised the first Ridgebacks. Their dull paintwork was seen, in the context of a society obsessed with understated design and packaging, as really cool and their price of £287 as really hot.

The following year a new UK company, Muddy Fox, imported twelve complete bikes from Japan, put them on a Welsh hillside and photographed them. They also photographed one machine suspended above a mirror-like lake to give it biblical dimensions. Both pictures were used in a huge advertising campaign through the cycle Press and were instrumental in making Muddy Fox the market leaders in the sale of mountain bikes.

For the few hundred mountain bikers in the UK 1984 was their chance to come out of the bike shed. The first national meeting was held at a cycle track in London, about as far removed from mountains and tranquillity as one could get. The Eastway event in April was followed by a meeting in rural Sussex which attracted 700 participants. Like the Eastway races, it favoured short-course scrambles which pleased the crowds and encouraged the sponsors.

Not everybody likes to race around dirt-tracks and the real essence of mountain biking – getting off the beaten track and into the wilderness – was fostered by the newly-launched National Off-Road Bicycle Association (UK), commonly known as NORBA. It was an imitator of an American outfit, but adapted to the more prosaic attitudes of British outdoor enthusiasts. NORBA took note of the conflict which mountain biking was inspiring in the US and so it published the *Off-Road Code* (see Chapter 4). It aimed to prevent bike riders from abusing the countryside and from making enemies of the powerful farming, horse-riding and walking lobbies. So far, it has succeeded.

Mountain biking grew slowly in the next two years. The media liked it, particularly when modern day adventurers tackled real mountains on their bikes. Ted Pearson cycled up Ben Nevis in 1984. John Moore scaled Mount Olympus. Three students cycled from Alaska to Chile. Two explorers entered China. The Crane cousins pedalled to the top of Kilimanjaro. The first mountain bike shop in the Himalayas was opened.

But despite the huge amount of publicity which these new machines received, there was no indication that they would sell *en masse* in the UK. The industry wanted another BMX boom but the punters were not clamouring like they should. The TV, newspaper and magazine reporters could not accept that £400 was a sensible price for a bicycle, not even in the days when conspicuous consumption and 'yuppies' ruled supreme.

It was the latter who finally clinched the popularity of mountain bikes in the UK. A mountain bike projected instant potential. The riders did not actually have to go anywhere near a mountain, the rugged bike simply conferred upon them an air of tough, independent, go-getting energy. So, ironically, mountain bikes first broke through in the cities and they stood for self-assertion. Since the days of the hobby-horse, bicycles have always been used for posing and mountain bikes became the latest in a long line of dandy-mobiles.

Mountain bike sport lay dormant in England in 1986 after the demise of the nationwide Fat Tyre Five series, though races did still take place in Scotland and Wales. The cycle industry failed to support events – they were spending their time and money on redesigning frame geometry, choosing new colour schemes and extolling the virtues of new components. Mountain bikes were becoming technical and there was a glut of trade literature which was full of the language usually associated with microchip technology. Even NORBA went into a coma and only awoke in January of the following year to stage its last ride before re-emerging as the Mountain Bike Club (see Directory, page 140).

This period of entrenchment produced good results. Holiday centres and training weekends for beginners sprang up wherever a tourist board grant was to be had and windsurfers decided that dry land and a pair of wheels instead of a sail had their advantages when the wind was low. Boy George bought a mountain bike. The British Olympic cross-country skiing squad bought mountain bikes. Shepherds, policemen and countryside wardens bought mountain bikes. They were everywhere.

In 1987 it was estimated that there were 50,000 mountain bikes on the road, off the road and sometimes in the hedges of Britain. It was not a great number compared to the one million new bikes sold every year, but a new leisure activity had come of age. In the US in 1984 mountain bikes accounted for one-tenth of all bikes sold and, three years later, this had risen to one-third. A similar growth in the UK would make mountain bikes the most popular breed of bicycle around.

That same year local clubs sprang up all over the country. They explored the bridleways and byways which had not seen a horse for donkey's years and they made creative use of derelict land. It was unfortunately also the year in which the first fatal mountain biking accident was reported – a tired rider fell from the pier of a demolished railway bridge in Argyll.

A short-course national championship was revived, to a mixed reception from riders who had competed among the real mountains in France at the first so-called World Championship. A second unofficial World Championship was held in the States and one day soon there may well be a single, official world title. In Britain the

Mountain biking is a sociable activity conducted at a civilised pace.

sport got official backing and sponsorship from giant Japanese component manufacturers Shimano.

For most mountain bikers this short history of racing and sales may seem irrelevant but it is an attempt to put in perspective the activity which has led to the development and design of those components which are used today. Tyre tread patterns have become as important as gear ratios in making a better bike. Sloping top tubes and shorter chainstays have improved the agility of the mountain bike. Sealed bearings have made it more reliable.

Mountain bikes will continue to evolve and mountain biking will become more and more enjoyable as a result, whether you are interested in racing, leisure riding or simply freewheeling down hills and pushing up the other side. All you have to do is saddle up and head towards yonder horizon. So go on, get off the road!

2 *Buying a Mountain Bike*

There is no point in buying a mountain bike unless you have some inkling about what kind of riding you enjoy and how to find a machine which will do it. Sure, the colour of the bike which the assistant is trying to sell matches your eyes perfectly and, by sheer coincidence, its price equals your credit rating – but these are not good enough reasons to buy. You have to know that the bike suits your purpose, you have to be sure that it is suitable for your wild adventures or your lazy rambles.

This chapter tells you everything you need to know before buying a mountain bike. If you have already bought one then you will glean useful tips on how to get even more from your bike. And if you have had enough of mountain biking and want to go back to train-spotting then you will learn all the right jargon for selling your second-hand machine.

What is a Mountain Bike?

There is no single perfect example of a mountain bike, so for definition's sake we will have to generalise. A common feature of mountain bikes is the 26 in-diameter wheels. Small models may have 24 in-wheels, while a few extraordinary machines mix the sizes front and back. All rims accept tyres which are fat, from 1.5 in to 2.25 in wide. The frames have a reasonably relaxed geometry, good ground clearance and flat, wide handlebars. They have up to 18 derailleur gears and the brakes are more powerful than ordinary calipers. Gear levers are mounted on the bars and so are the motorcycle-style brake levers.

This mix of components means that mountain bikes are more stable, safer and stronger than other breeds. They are suitable for riding on difficult and dangerous roads and for riding over rough ground. Some mountain bikes are built with a lot of road use in mind, while others are built purely for off-road racing. And in between there is a whole host of variations.

So you have to decide why you want a mountain bike. We all know that it is a cool and trendy thing, but how will you use it and where will you ride? It is estimated that over 90 per cent of mountain bikes spend over 90 per cent of their time on surfaced roads, but it is that missing 10 per cent, the times when you quit the tarmac and get off the beaten track, that a mountain bike really comes into its own. First you must judge how much time you will spend off the road.

Your Kind of Riding

A top mountain bike is over-equipped and over-designed to be used purely as a road machine. To be brutally honest, if you are into road racing, long-distance cycle-touring or short shopping trips then a mountain bike is a waste of money. There are ordinary bicycles which perform those functions more economically and more efficiently. But take it off the road for, say, an average of an hour a week and a budget mountain bike will give you your money's worth. It will let you ride that towpath you never dared follow. It will carry you up forgotten lanes. It will have at least ten gears, fat tyres, a conventional mountain bike frame, mudguards and a rack.

A budget urban mountain bike such as this is a tuned-up version of your great-grandmother's roadster. The lowest of the ten gears will get you up steep hills, if the legs are willing, and will just drive you to the top of short off-road climbs. The tyres will have a central ridge to make riding on tarmac less tiring, though off-road the same ridge will not grip as well as more knobbly tyres. The frame and fork will have a relaxed geometry so that steering is stable but positive. The brakes will probably be cantilevers, front and back, but could be one of several other high-tech designs. The gear mechanisms may be indexed, that is, linked to the gear levers so that one click on the lever means the gear will change by one cog. With all these gizmos it is a very serviceable bike and, with care, will last many years.

It is highly probable that you will find your urban mountain bike a real boon in towns. The upright riding position allows you to see over traffic, the fat tyres bounce through pot-holes, the conveniently-located control levers inspire confidence and the strong brakes pull you up short of disaster. It may even inspire you to try something a little more racy, a real off-road mountain bike.

If you pay a little bit more money you can buy a machine with 15 or 18 gears, all indexed for easy shifting, and with a slightly lighter frame which has steeper head tube and seat tube angles. The brakes will be exotic at the back, probably U-brakes or Roller-cams (see below). The tyres will be knobbly to grip in the mud. The rack and the mudguards will not be fitted as standard items. Most of the bearings of the moving parts, such as the hubs and the bottom bracket (where the pedal cranks enter the frame) will be 'sealed' to stop the grease from escaping.

All these changes make for a tougher, more manœuvrable machine so that it is easier to hop over and around natural obstacles. A real off-road mountain bike will not sap your energy as quickly as an urban version. It is lighter and more co-operative when it comes up against the rough stuff. You can, of course, also use an off-road mountain bike on the road.

What if you are really hooked? You spend all day riding the hills, looking for new challenges and neglecting your duties. The time is right to buy a top-flight machine which could cost up to six times the price of an urban mountain bike. An expert's bike may be 'off-the-peg', at the top of an established mass-producer's range, in which case you are actually getting a bargain. Mass-producers buy vast numbers of components at low prices and so they can afford to fit the best to their top models without raising prices dramatically. If you opt for a custom-built mountain bike from one of the hundreds of small framebuilders in the UK you will get as close to the perfect machine as is possible. The frame will fit you exactly and should have the smartest components around. You will be able to specify the number and type of gears, the length of the pedal cranks, the frame geometry, even the exact location of the water bottle cage. Anything is possible.

In general, a top mountain bike will have many extras permanently brazed to the frame. It will have bosses for bottle cage, pump-pegs and cable guides. It will have quick-release wheels. All bearings will be sealed. All components will be aluminium alloy. And the paintwork will match your eyes!

A Bike that Fits

New mountain bikes cost from £150 for a small-framed urban model and up to £5,000 for a 22 carat gold-plated and carbon-fibre piece of art. Our recommendation is to think carefully about where and how often you will ride your mountain bike and understand a smattering of the technical jargon before choosing.

Buy a mountain bike that fits you. Do not be tempted to buy the first machine you see. Be prepared to wait until your shop has got the right size bike in stock. A bike which fits badly will be a pain to ride – literally. The stress can damage your knees, back and wrists permanently. The type of riding involved when cycling off-road puts more strain on your back and shoulders so it is essential to get a mountain bike which fits. If you are not looking for a custom-built machine, simply measure your inside leg, divide it by three, double that and subtract 2 in. So someone with an inside leg of 30 in should buy a mountain bike with a frame of 18 in ($30/3 = 10$, $10 \times 2 = 20$, $20 - 2 = 18$).

Choosing a Frame

You will need to know a little about the frame and about the components so here are a few of the more interesting points.

Mountain bike frames are made of different metals. The least expensive are made of plain steel tubes and either they will bear a sticker which says so or they will be totally anonymous. Steel tubes need to be thick to be strong enough to withstand the battering they get when made into a rip-roaring mountain bike. It is this extra thickness which makes steel frames the heaviest. The heavier the bike, the more of your energy it consumes.

Steel alloy tubes are stronger than plain steel. A frame made of a steel alloy will announce itself clearly by a sticker, usually on one of the main tubes. There are several different specialist manufacturers of alloy tubing, they include Reynolds, Columbus, Tange, Ishiwata and Vitus; and to confuse matters there are also

several different types of alloy and several different kinds of
fabrication.

The most common steel alloy used on mountain bikes is chrome
molybdenum, known in the trade as cro-moly or cro-mo. It proved
its worth on BMX bikes and is seen as a good, reasonably light and

*A 'mixte' frame mountain bike makes getting on and off easier but the frame
can be more flexible and heavier than a conventional 'diamond' frame
mountain bike.*

responsive tubing. A good cro-moly tube will be seamless, it will have been drawn from metal blanks at the rolling mill and will probably be 'butted'. A butted tube is one which has different wall thicknesses along its length. By changing the thickness of a tube wall the tube is made strong at the required points, usually at each end, and light at the points where strength is not needed. The most common cro-mo tubes are double butted along their length which means the wall has two different thicknesses along its length. The most expensive are triple butted to save even more weight, and heat treated to make them even stronger. You will not be able to see the butting on a frame tube, because the variations are made on the inside, but you will be able to see the sticker which announces the extent of the butting. The stickers are produced and strictly controlled by the tubing manufacturers, not the framebuilders, and on new bikes they can be trusted.

The next step up is manganese molybdenum steel alloy, the most common being Reynolds 531. It is an alloy which has been used by bicycle manufacturers for more than 50 years and requires a lot of care when being built into a frame. For that reason it is not as suitable for automated mass-production and is favoured mainly by custom framebuilders. Manganese molybdenum frames are as strong, sometimes lighter and usually longer-lasting than cro-moly frames. They too will be butted internally.

A few frames have been made from very light steel alloys such as Reynolds 753, from aerodynamic tubing, from carbon fibre and from oval cross-section tubing, but if you are considering such extravagances you would do well to talk to a custom framebuilder for individual advice. After all, such tubes announce that you have spent a lot so you might as well get your money's worth.

A final word on steel alloy frame stickers – read the small print. It might say that only the three main tubes of the bicycle frame are made of the alloy, in which case you can bet the smaller tubes that hold the rear wheel are made of plain steel. On the other hand, a better frame will have a sticker which states that all tubes are made of the relevant alloy.

Aluminium

Aluminium is a newcomer to bicycle frames of all species and has been particularly popular among mountain bikes thanks to

Cannondale in the US and to Kettler in Germany. You can spot an aluminium frame because its tubes are even fatter than usual. Aluminium is lighter than steel alloy but is not as strong. Doubling the diameter of the tube makes it eight times stronger. It also increases the weight to the same as that of a steel alloy frame. On road bikes there have been claims that the extra stiffness transmits too many jolts to the rider but on mountain bikes the tyres affect the comfort of the ride more than the frame does. Aluminium frames stand out among a herd of mountain bikes and catch the eye.

Casing the Joints

You should also take note of the way in which the frame tubes are joined together. Traditionally steel alloy frames have used 'lugs'. A lug is a piece of metal shaped into sleeves to receive tube ends. When bronze or silver solder inside the sleeve is heated and allowed to cool (a technique called 'brazing') the tube ends become fixed into the lug.

Welding has become a more popular form of framebuilding. The tubes are melted together by a tungsten-tipped torch in an environment of inert gas to prevent inclusions. This is known as TIG (tungsten inert gas) welding. TIG welds have no external sleeves and may show a ring of melt ripples around the join. The neater and more consistent the ripples, the better the join. All aluminium frames are TIG-welded.

All framebuilders try to make their frames as attractive as cost will permit so tube joins are cleaned up by filing away extraneous pieces of brazing metal and weld ripples. Some create seamless-looking joins by filing away all the weld ripples, or filling the gap with a fillet of bronze.

The Fork and Crown

Take a look at the front fork next, the pair of long blades which hold the front wheel. It has a crown where the blades join and enter the vertical steering tube. The crown is a victim of fashion and its style changes regularly. One season the favourite will be gracefully-curved Uni-crown forks, the next season the clever money will be on sloping-crown forks and, one day, even flat-top crowns will rise again. No single type of crown has been shown to have any strength advantage over any other, though the TIG-welded styles are cheaper to make in mass production and some designs give greater clearance for fatter tyres.

The fork blades themselves may not be made of the same metal as the frame. If the frame sticker does not mention the fork and if there is no sticker on the crown or on either of the blades then they are definitely made of plain steel.

There is something to be said for having a fork set which is of a cheaper metal than the frame because forks take a lot of punishment and are the frame component most likely to become damaged. Bent forks can often be straightened and, if not, they can be replaced cheaply. On the other hand, a bent frame is frequently irreparable and it costs an arm and a leg to replace. So it makes sense to treat forks as sacrificial components to protect both frame and rider from the full force of sudden impacts.

The 'finish' of a frame and fork set can be inspected closely at the bike shop. Look for the degree of care which has gone into filing the joints and the evenness of the paint. A well-finished frame will be silky smooth, around all brazes and welds. The paint will be even, even in the most inaccessible places. Painting can either be enamel, epoxy coating or electrostatically sprayed. Baked epoxy powder coating is the most durable.

The Right Shape for the Right Ride

The geometry of a mountain bike frame largely determines the quality of the ride. The first models to appear in the UK were long, loping machines which zoomed down hills like Sherman tanks. Unfortunately, they needed a Sherman tank to tow them back up again. That is because their geometry was extremely stable. The key elements are the angles of the seat tube and the head tube. The seat tube holds the saddle pillar and the head tube holds the handlebar stem, the steering column and the fork. On old roadsters both these tubes were fixed at about 69 degrees from the horizontal. By combining this with a rake, or forward bend, in the front fork blades of up to 2.5 in, an old roadster was extremely willing to hold a straight line and hard work to turn suddenly to left or right. The relaxed seat tube angle also meant that the frame absorbed a lot of the road shock before it reached the saddle.

The first mountain bikes copied this pattern, while racing bikes

were experimenting with angles as steep as 75 degrees. The steeper
the angles and the shorter the fork rake, the closer the two wheels
become. This makes the steering more nimble, the rider less stable
and the road shocks more bruising. Mountain bikes, like all other
bikes, will always be victims of experiments with frame angles but
the current favourite for off-road models is to have a seat tube angle
of about 71 degrees and a head angle of about 72 degrees with a
rake of 2 in. This is a huge generalisation but can be used as a guide
for a reasonably sedate mountain bike which has enough agility to
make successfully steering up steep hills easy. Of course, these
measurements will vary with the overall size of the frame and the
intended use of the bike. For a more stable ride go for a more
shallow frame, for a twitchy ride go for something steeper.

A final few words on frames (if you are riveted by this subject
then there are entire books devoted to it). Many of the sporty
mountain bikes have sloping top tubes which give more knee room
when you are standing on the pedals and hammering round a
corner. They allow you to tilt the bike without risk to your kneebones
or your crutch. There are a few 'mixte' or 'ladies' frames around
for those who do not like top tubes (crossbars) and they are slightly
heavier and more prone to flexing.

Pedals

Mountain bike pedals should give good grip and they come in two
main types – platform and bear trap. Platform pedals do not grip
as well as bear traps but neither do they sink their teeth into your
shins as bear traps have a tendency to do. Some pedals contain
'sealed' bearings which is no bad thing as they are frequently being
stuck in the mud and water. Platforms tend to be made of nylon
resin while bear traps are of metal.

Cranks

The pedals are attached to cranks, which can range from 165 mm
to 175 mm. If the bottom bracket (the lowest part of the frame, see
below) is under 11 in off the ground, choose shorter cranks otherwise
the pedals may catch the ground when cornering at speed. Also, bear
in mind that you will probably wear wide shoes when mountain
biking and a bulbous crank may rub them annoyingly on each

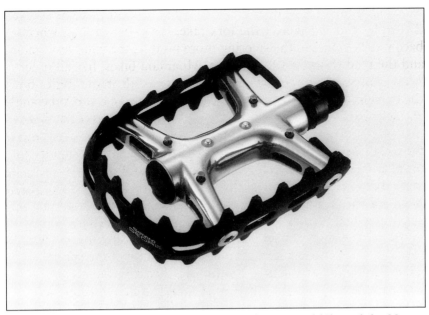

Pedals are always wider and tougher than ordinary road bike pedals. Many have removable outer toothed cages which can be replaced when worn or damaged.

revolution. The cheapest cranks are made separately from the 'spider' which holds the chainrings; better versions have forged one-piece cranks and spiders.

Chainrings

The crankset holds the chainrings, either two or three toothed rings which transmit your pedalling energy to the chain. Until 1984 chainrings were circular. Since then many of them have become squashed circles. Each manufacturer uses different jargon to explain their squashed circle but the upshot is the same – they make pedalling easier. Your leg can deliver most power to the pedals when the pedal cranks are past the vertical. At the moment when the pedals are actually vertical you can't deliver any useful energy. The squashed circle chainrings diminish the problems of this stop-go-stop-go cycle by reducing the time the cranks spend in the near-vertical region each revolution and by increasing the time they spend in the useful region. Sounds complicated? Well, just try understanding the conflicting arguments from the manufacturers.

The best way to judge their effect is to ride with a squashed circle chainring. Its benefit is most noticeable when cycling in a very low gear up a very steep track.

Chainrings come in plain steel or in aluminium alloy. Alloy is lighter and more expensive though slightly more prone to damage. Chainrings, being very close to the ground, are vulnerable to obstacles and, indeed, if you get addicted to log-climbing you will use the chainrings to dig into the log and pull you over (see Front Wheel Techniques, Chapter 3). If your front derailleur is indexed the chainring will be plain steel because the teeth are more resistant to the battering they get from indexed changing. The cheapest steel chainrings are stamped from a sheet of metal. Better alloy rings are cast and ground which makes them more accurate and less likely to wear the chain.

Bottom Bracket

The chainset is attached, by a steel spindle, to the bottom bracket shell of the bicycle frame. The set of bearings inside the bottom bracket of a mountain bike takes the heaviest pounding of any moving part of any bicycle. It is not a lot to look at from the outside but inside it is a swirling mass of ball bearings, grease and, very often, dirt. On a reasonable bike these bearings should be sealed or shielded to stop the grease from making a quick getaway and dirt a rapid entry. The brochure will say if the bearing is sealed, if it does not say so then you can assume it is not sealed. Any dirt inside a bottom bracket will soon erode the bearings and the unit will start crunching and grinding until eventually it gives up. You will then need a new bottom bracket unit and possibly a new spindle. It would be better to clean the unit regularly (see Chapter 5 for details).

Chain

Chains come in standard widths and like most vital cycle components, you get what you pay for. Finer machining tolerances, less play and easier changing-performance all cost money. Some chains have bent or shaped links but in practice these do not make a whole heap of difference. Do not expect a mountain bike chain to last more than a year of rough stuff even when kept clean and well lubricated.

Non-circular chainrings look crazy but their fans swear by them. They are designed to make pedalling easier and more efficient.

Sprockets, Block and Freewheel

The chain transmits your power to the rear cluster of five or six sprockets. These are made of steel and have teeth which are often contoured and twisted slightly to accept the chain more easily when the gear is changed. The sprockets fit on to a freewheel block and can be swapped to produce different gear ratios. The freewheel block is a complex piece of equipment which fits on to the wheel hub. Basically, it allows the chain to drive the wheel forward but it does not allow the wheel to drive the chain forward. This means you can whizz downhill without the pedals shooting round like propeller blades.

Wheels

The wheels are very strong. On all but the cheapest mountain bikes the rims will be made of aluminium alloy. In fact, plain steel rims

Quick release levers on wheel hubs can make wheel changes very easy but they can also help opportunist thieves.

are a positive danger on a mountain bike because brake pads do not grip well in the wet, and you can bet that your wheels will get wet when riding off-road. Alloy rims are slightly less shiny in appearance than steel and are often 'anodised', a treatment which increases their strength and corrosion-resistance.

Mountain bike wheels are stronger than ordinary cycle wheels because they have to be. This is achieved in several ways. The diameter is slightly smaller, just 26 in compared to 27 in. The rim is wider, at 1.25 in. Often the flange of the hub is wide to reduce the length of the spokes and increase the shock-absorbing factor. The spokes are of a heavier gauge, known as 14 g.

Apart from checking how true a wheel is, by spinning it and seeing whether it runs in line compared to the position of the brake pads, you should try squeezing the spokes to see if they are in even tension all the way round. The hub of a wheel takes a battering almost as heavy as the bottom bracket unit of the frame, so aim for a quality hub.

Tyres

Tyres are evolving a science of their own and, after the frame, a mountain bike tyre has the greatest effect on the quality of the ride.

So when you are buying a brand new machine for the first time you should be aware of a few points. The fatter the tyre the heavier it is and the harder it is to pedal. Tyres range from 1.5 in- to 2.25 in- wide. A fat rear tyre may rub a close-fitting frame and also can have a tendency to catch the chain and trap it under the chainstay. A narrow tyre with a central rib is supposed to make light work of road riding but will not grip well off the road. The softer the rubber compound the better the tyre will grip on rocky surfaces but the sooner it will wear out. The more knobbles on a tyre the better it will grip on soft surfaces but the more of your energy it will absorb on flat surfaces. A heavily used and well-maintained tyre could last up to three years if ridden mostly on road, or one year if taken up rocky tracks constantly.

Inner Tubes and Valves

One of the best things about a mountain bike is the relatively small number of punctures. The fat tyres are good at resisting sharp objects. However, the occasional puncture is inevitable. That is when you will notice that your pump does not fit your tyre valve.

There are three types of valve – Woods, Shraeder and Presta. Woods are very old-fashioned but still found on the odd mountain bike. Heaven only knows why, possibly they are very cheap. Shraeder valves are identical to those on car tyres and so you can inflate them with a car foot pump as well as bicycle pump with the correct adaptor. Never use compressed air-lines at garages because they can blow the tyre to smithereens in front of, and at close quarters to, your face. Presta valves, sometimes called high-pressure or HP, are distinguished by having a small metal spigot sticking out of the centre with a silver metal cap which unscrews and wobbles about. Take a look under the dust cap to see if you have the flat, fat Shraeder or the slim, spiky Presta. For mountain biking neither valve has any great advantage, but make sure that both inner tubes and all your spares have the same type and that the pump matches.

Gear Mechanisms

Now we come to the gear mechanisms, sometimes called derailleurs or gear mechs. The gear levers on the handlebars are sometimes called gear shifters or thumbshifters to increase the confusion.

Anyway, there are up to twenty makes of mountain bike gear mechanisms and each has several different models. The rear mech lifts up the chain and moves it across to be in line with the next sprocket. Then it drops it on to the sprocket and you will feel pretty smug because you have just completed a smooth, silent gear change. The rear mech also takes up any slack in the chain.

Gear mechanisms on mountain bikes get a rough ride. Firstly, they have to carry the chain across a wide range of different sized sprockets, lifting it bodily up and down wide steps while the chain is still rattling through the derailleur cage. Secondly, they have to take up an awful lot of slack, particularly when the chain is resting on the smallest chainring and sprocket. And they have to do this a few inches above flying boulders and splashing mud. The dozens of tiny components which make up a gear mech have to be sensitive to the commands they receive from the gear lever via the gear cable, and resistant to the muck and hammering from the trail below. It is hardly surprising they are the most common source of problems.

When you are buying your first mountain bike look for one which has indexed gears. They have a special mechanism which links one click on the gear lever to a change of one sprocket by the rear mech. So gear changing is very simple. Click and change all the way. However, indexed gears are slightly more expensive than non-indexed, or 'friction' as they are sometimes called. Friction derailleurs require a little more skill and judgement with your thumb pressure on the gear lever but they can be just as effective and even quicker once you are familiar with them.

Long-cage derailleurs are more vulnerable to damage than short-cage models because they hang closer to the ground. There is also more danger that they will 'wrap up' into the spokes and bring you to a sudden stop. But long-cage derailleurs can handle a very wide range of sprocket sizes with ease and still take up all the slack chain. If you want a wide range of gears, from very low to very high, a long-cage is essential.

The front gear mechanism is simpler because it does not take up any slack, it simply shoves the chain from chainring to chainring. Indexed versions are so positive that the chainrings must be of tough steel to withstand the extra wear.

Gear mechanisms are using increasing amounts of resin or plastic components but on the whole they are made of pressed steel or more expensive aluminium alloy. They may have sealed-bearing jockey wheels and smooth styling but you get what you pay for and an expensive mountain bike should have the top-line gear mechs.

The most expensive front gear mech is the Browning Automatic and it works in a different way. A segment of the middle of the three front chainrings is hinged. It carries the chain from one ring to the next, like a set of railway points. In engineering terms it is more efficient, in financial terms it is mind-boggling.

Rear derailleurs do not feature on some mountain bikes, instead they have hub gears, like on shopping bikes. The advantage of hub gears is that they are not affected by mud, being well-protected at the very centre of the wheel. However, the range of gears they offer is greatly limited, and should you ever require a new rear wheel you will have to have it specially built up with the old hub gear.

Brakes

Good brakes are vital to good mountain biking. Don't go off road if you have a machine which is fitted with a pair of pressed-steel caliper brakes which squeeze the rim like wet cotton wool. Bad brakes could kill you.

The most common form of brakes are rim brakes and the most common of these are cantilevers. Nearly all mountain bikes have cantilever front brakes. They are inexpensive, extremely efficient and easy to maintain. Nothing less than a cantilever brake can deliver sufficient stopping force to the rim of a mountain bike. The pivoted brake-pad holder multiplies the pressure applied to the brake lever.

Cantilevers used to be the most common rear brakes but they have been superseded by more powerful and exotic designs which, because of their strength, have to be attached underneath the chainstay tubes (except on oversized or strengthened tubes). Models such as the Shimano U-brake and the Suntour Rollercam give more powerful braking.

Brakes are made of pressed plain steel or cast aluminium alloy or nylon resin. The nature of the brake pads affects stopping power and synthetic pads stop better, though they can cause greater rim wear. If you have the misfortune to ride steel rims, then leather-faced brake blocks are your safest bet.

Hub brakes are favoured by some riders because they are not affected by mud and water. They are slightly heavier than an

Nylon resin cantilever brakes use a steel chassis to combine strength with light weight.

Cantilever brakes have been fitted to mountain bikes since the Californian prototypes. Neat, fully adjustable, easy to maintain and powerful, they continue to be the most popular braking systems for off-road bikes.

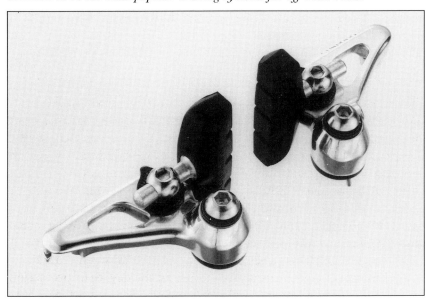

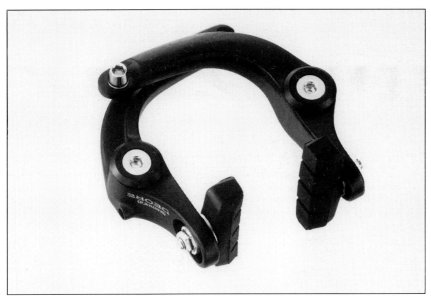

U-brakes have replaced rear cantilevers on many bikes. Their biggest advantage is that they do not foul the luggage on a rear rack.

equivalent rim brake but they are far stronger. They also make a rear wheel stronger because they have very wide flanges. However, just as with hub gears, should you require a new rear wheel after an accident, one would have to be built up specially using the old hub brake or a replacement.

Gear and Brake Levers

The gears and brakes are controlled by levers mounted on the handlebars. Some mountings combine the two levers but separate mountings are preferable because they give you maximum flexibility. They can be positioned separately to fit your hands and they can be replaced when you want to upgrade individual components. Different brake levers suit differently shaped hands but take note of the reach of the lever. If the gap between the lever and the handlebar is too long your hand will get tired quickly on long, steep descents. The reach of some better levers can be adjusted.

Thumbshifters themselves do not vary much between brands, but the material of which they are made and the degree of protection they are afforded by the integral cowling does. It is traditional that

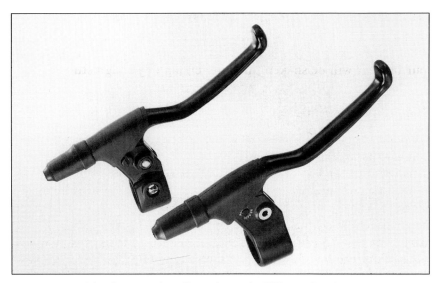

Brake levers like these can be adjusted to suit different hand sizes. Good quality levers have rounded ends to prevent injuries in a crash.

the rear gear mech lever is on the right and the front mech lever is on the left of the handlebar, so that your left hand can apply the rear brake while your right thumb changes down through the gears. If the gears are indexed then the thumbshifter should also have a switch to convert them back to friction mode.

Handlebars

Handlebars come in different shapes, all with silly names like the bullmoose, the slingshot, the swan-neck, the one-piece, the two-piece and, if it became fashionable, the three-piece suite. Basically, the handlebar is wide to give good leverage when steering. Narrower bars are preferred by very experienced riders and by urban mountain bikers who squeeze through traffic jams. Bars are usually plain steel or aluminium, occasionally an expensive bike will have steel alloy bars and, even more rare, they may have carbon-fibre bars.

Stem

Stem design changes every couple of years but now there is a growing awareness of the importance of the stem in making a mountain bike which fits the rider. The rise and the reach of the stem combine to affect how far forward a rider has to lean to hold the handlebar grips. Buy a bike which does not put undue stress on your back, it will be shaken up badly enough by rough stuff.

Handgrips and Saddle

The comfort of a mountain bike, you will appreciate, comes mostly from the handlebar grips and the saddle. Foam or thick rubber grips take out the last jolts of road, or off-road, shock. Foam grips act like sponges in wet weather and rubber grips mark the wallpaper – but never leave home without them. Saddles are a particularly personal item and no two people can agree on this fundamental issue. The key point to remember is: don't worry if the saddle hurts for the first week. If, however, after a couple of months it still brings tears to your eyes you should exchange it (or see a doctor). The seat pin beneath is plain steel on cheap bikes and aluminium alloy on the more expensive models. All saddles have rails beneath them. On better bikes, these fit into a micro-adjust clamp which can be adjusted fore and aft for perfect positioning as well as for a comfortable seating angle.

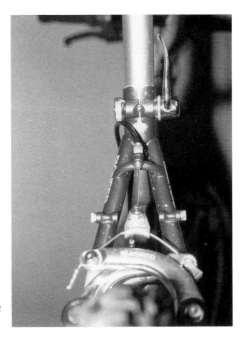

The back end, showing the quick-release seat bolt, rear brake cable adjuster and mounting points for a four-point rack.

A complete groupset of components, like this Shimano Deore, is not cheap but will ensure that all components work well together. This is particularly important with indexed gear systems and the new generation of brakes.

Optional Extras

There are a few other accessories you will come across when choosing your wilderness steed. There may be a quick-release lever on the top of the seat tube, to release the saddle post. This is useful for altering your centre of gravity when swooping down hills and steaming up the other side, but it also helps thieves steal your saddle in town. Similarly, quick-release (Q/R) wheels save time when fixing punctures or stowing the bike in the back of a car but they too assist thieves. Gear and brake cable sleeves may be internally Teflon-coated to reduce friction. Mudguards, pumps, water bottle cages and pannier racks may be fitted as standard but only you will know how useful they will be. Don't let a few free extras fool you into buying a duff mountain bike. Take your time choosing. A good mountain bike is a transport of delight.

3 How to Ride your Mountain Bike

You are now one of the lucky ones. You own a mountain bike. The time has come to get more closely acquainted with this new friend. You need to get your act together, literally. Time to ride the wild turf.

First of all, you must make sure that your bike and you understand each other. You can only do this if you are comfortable. The bars and saddle obviously need to be set at their most convenient adjustments. The brake levers should all fall easily and instinctively to hand as soon as you start to move, ready for action if you need a rapid stop. The gear shift levers should allow a harmonious understanding between pedal action and finger movement. To coin a phrase, the bike should be 'set up' to complement you and your riding style.

Setting up

First set the saddle height to a comfortable position by unlocking the quick-release (Q/R) seat bolt and pulling the saddle up to higher than you think it needs to be. Then sit on the bike. Loosen the seat bolt slightly and let the saddle sink down until you can just touch the ground with the tips of your toes. Your saddle height will now be OK for starters, but you might find that you want to raise it slightly once you have gained more confidence and experience. The old chestnut that you should be able to touch the ground easily with

both feet does not apply to many mountain bikes, so don't think
you have got it wrong if you prefer a higher setting. Ideally, your
knee should be slightly bent when your foot is at the bottom of the
pedal stroke, irrespective of saddle-ground distance. The front of
the saddle should be slightly higher than the back for maximum
comfort and stability and this can be adjusted by means of the
micro-adjust clamp under the seat pillar mount.

Next, set the bars to the most comfortable position. If you have
got one-piece bars raise them as high as they will go. If they are
two-piece try to fix them so that you can grip comfortably without
leaning too far forward. When you are learning, you will be tense
enough anyway, so don't put any extra strain or weight on your
wrists than you can possibly manage. Your bum will be happy to
accept a little more responsibility to begin with; when you are into
the racing team you can move your riding position forward if you
want. Don't think you have to look like the head-down riders' photos
you see in the racing magazines. They are being paid to be in pain,
you are not. You are learning for the pleasure of it, so sit up and
enjoy.

Now you are seated comfortably, make sure the controls are easy
to get at. You should be able to grip both brake levers without
having to stretch. Ideally, you should be able to operate the levers
with the two middle fingers of each hand. If not, many levers have
a reach adjustment to bring them closer to the bars. If there is no
reach adjustment, try moving the levers in or out along the bars so
that they curve more towards the grips. If all this fails, get your
levers changed. You *need* to get to your brake levers – no excuses
will make up for a crunched front-end and face if you can't stop
when you need to.

When you have adjusted the levers for reach, make sure they are
angled down, around 45 degrees. This makes it easier to work the
brakes when you are standing up on the pedals, and makes it less
likely that you will trap your fingers when crashing through narrow
gaps. Move the gear shift levers (if they need it) as close as you can
to the inside edge of the brake levers, so that you can easily move
them through the whole arc required to change from top to bottom
gears. You should be able to do this without having to shift your
hand position. A slight downward tilt often helps make them easier
to operate.

So you are ready to go. You are now, as we said earlier, closely acquainted and comfortable, just as you should be. Assuming you are wearing the right sort of clothing – gloves, long socks and as much padding as you can muster without becoming a ball of sweat – go to it.

Braking

Just a moment though; making the bike stop is always more tricky than making it go, so first have a look at how you go about the arresting process. Better now than halfway down the side of a quarry, with all the other worries about life insurance crowding for space in your brain.

With such powerful braking systems as are now the standard on mountain bikes, care must be exercised in their application. If you simply grab a handful of both brake levers you will surely lock up both wheels, and probably skid and fall off. Both levers should be used with some degree of gentility. If you lock both wheels up, you will probably take longer to stop than if you keep them almost, but not quite, skidding. That is why motor car manufacturers make such a big thing of anti-lock braking systems – they do stop cars quicker.

Common sense tells us that whatever brake pressure you decide to use, the front brake should always get a little bit less than the back. If you slow the front wheel more than the back, one of two things will happen. Either the whole bike will tip up on the front wheel axle and throw you over the bars, or the front wheel will skid. Either way, you will suddenly lose steering control and probably crash. However, if you adjust the cable tension so that the front brake only just locks the front wheel with the lever touching the bars you help avoid both of the above, even in a panic situation. The back brake can be set to whatever you like – a back wheel skid is easily corrected. If you like doing skid turns and buying new tyres regularly then set it for maximum grab. Otherwise set it to lock the wheel at about half travel.

Gearing

When you first start riding a mountain bike the temptation is to feel that, as you have such a formidable array of gears to choose from, it doesn't really matter which one you are in. This approach is just not good enough for readers of this book. As the owner of a highly technical machine, you should be taking a highly technical approach to gearing.

You will probably find that you are initially trying to push too high a gear (in an attempt to make the bike go too fast), so that when you come to a hill, some mud or a hidden ditch, you have to change down frantically through lots of gears to get to a manageable ratio. Usually you will find the poor rear gear mechanism giving in under the pressure, refusing to change and you, the rider, will fall off. This problem is not so common for those lucky riders who have index-shifting systems, but even so the chain-life will be shortened by this kind of reckless gear changing.

The sensible thing is to pedal in a fairly low gear, to keep the pedals spinning, rather than heaving on them. This has the advantage of placing you in the position where you can apply short bursts of high power easily without popping your kneecaps off under the pressure or crunching the gears. As riding away from the smooth predictability of tarmac often requires sudden action, you need to be ready for anything. Not only are you capable of getting out of trouble, mud, or both, more easily if you ride lower gears, but you will be able to change down faster if you are already in a low gear to start with.

As a rough guide to gearing: use the outer chainring only for riding on the road, or on very fast long downhill tracks where you want to see a parting in your hair. The middle and/or inner chainring should be used almost exclusively for off-road riding, although very steep hill-roads might need a very low gear if you are carrying a lot of luggage. It is usually best to choose a front chainring for a particular terrain and then stick to it, using the rear gears to give you the best speed-to-traction ratio.

One thing to remember is that although you have some very low gears at your disposal, they will not necessarily get you up the steepest hills or through the boggiest ditches. The use of very low gears can in some instances be exactly the wrong thing to do. The other important part of the equation when out riding is the amount of grip your tyres can get. So it is pointless riding straight at a very steep hill covered with small loose stones in your lowest gear. The back wheel will simply spin out and you will lose traction, momentum and face. You must learn to gauge the amount of grip you can get from any surface, and gear accordingly.

Slippery or loose surfaces are best approached using a medium gear rather than a low one, say small front chainring and first or second smallest sprocket on the freewheel. But if the surface is firm and grippy, the lower the gear you can get the better your chances of conquering the obstacle. Some riders deflate the rear tyre slightly to give more grip, but it doesn't always work. The occurrence of firm, grippy hill-surfaces is unfortunately not particularly common, so you often find yourself looking at a fairly steep yet slippery hill and wondering what on earth to do. The trick is to go fast.

If you are approaching an obstacle for which techno-logic tells you that you will require a low gear, try to gain as much speed as you can prior to actually reaching it. Psycho-logic will show you that your own momentum will carry you well into, up, over or through the tricky bit. Try it with both steep hills and muddy patches. The advantages are that you will be going faster and therefore be able to balance better, you will be in a higher gear and therefore liable to less wheelspin, and you will be able to gain your initial momentum before the tricky section starts. Once you are through the worst, you can change down to give your legs a rest. That is what those low gears are really for.

Stand and Deliver

You have now mastered the art of plunging down steep river banks in a high gear so that your momentum carries you half-way across the torrent before you need to change down. If, or, more optimistically, when you make it to the other side you will be in a very low gear as you ready yourself and your bike for the climb out up the opposite bank. Ignoring the fact that your tyres will be dripping wet and less likely to grip than before their brief bath, you will hit a very steep slope with a large amount of torque, or twisting power, available at your rear wheel because of the low gear you are in. The effect of this torque can give one of two final results. Either your wheel will grip, and twist itself against the river bank so moving the whole bike up and out of the river. Or the wheel will grip, keep stationary and twist the whole bike up into the air around its axle, throwing you off the back of the bike into the water.

The way to avoid this involuntary bucking bronco sequence is to keep your weight where you can control it – firmly between the wheel axles. And so, to allow you to move your body around rapidly

to keep your weight central, you must learn to stand up on the pedals, whether freewheeling or pedalling, and regardless of ground conditions. Once you have accustomed yourself to not sitting down on the saddle during manœuvres, you will find you have achieved a new freedom – a feeling of competence.

To return to the river bank. If you stand up and lean forward as you go up it, you will be able to use the maximum torque you can generate at the rear wheel without the fear of flicking yourself off the back. You will inevitably find that you will need to practise to get the balance right, but after a few tries you will find it almost second nature and will be able to keep stable on some very steep slopes.

Likewise, if you are plunging down the river bank – or any steep hill come to that – and you decide you want to stop by applying

Opposite Climbing is a matter of speed or gearing. Either way, you need to keep your weight well forward to avoid back flips.

Very steep hills can be descended if you have got the nerve and the right stance.

the front brake, you will have a large amount of negative torque available at the front wheel trying to stop it turning. If the tyre grips, it can either slow the bike, or throw you suddenly over the front wheel into the water. If you are clever and keep your weight towards the back of the bike, you are unlikely to be thrown into the drink, and more likely to stop as you originally intended. It obviously makes sense to use the back brake more than the front, but the principle of keeping your weight central remains the same.

Even if the bike goes out of your control, you are more likely to be able to correct the problem if your weight is vertically between the front and rear wheel axles. You will get more traction, the steering will be more positive and, if you want, you will still be able to jump off the bike in a controlled fashion.

Getting off

Take a terminal downhill situation. If your weight is well back and you are hanging off the back of the saddle whilst fighting for control, you can simply put your feet down, let go of the bars and the bike will rush on uncontrollably without you, while you sit helplessly watching it. At least you won't get dented that way. If you try to cling on you will probably end up crashing badly with the bike landing on top of you. Nasty.

It can be equally unpleasant trying to get off the bike when you have decided that you are not going to make it to the top of that next rise, especially if your weight is not between the axles. When you grind to a halt and try to put your foot down, you find that the slope conspires against you. What should be terra firma a mere 30 in below your saddle in now thin air. The angle of the slope puts your groping foot another 6 in or so above the dirt, causing you to grip the brakes futilely as you hop backwards down the hill, until you trip and the bike lands on top of you once more. It has happened hundreds of time, is amusing to watch but very painful to experience at firsthand. Avoid it if you can.

All you need to do when you realise that you are not going to make it to the top, is to stand up on the pedals – if you are not already doing so – and lean right forwards over the bars. Some top tube padding makes this less potentially painful. You are now in a position to put one foot down where it will touch the ground, but you will probably still slither back down the hill even so. The extra

vital manœuvre is to turn the wheel sharply to the right, and put
your left foot down, or vice versa. The effect is to turn the bike
across the face of the slope, so that you can touch your foot down
above the bike. It sounds easy and it *is*, as long as you can remember
to do it.

In any situation where you think you are going to fall off, always
try to push the bike away and, if possible, in front of you so that the
effect is to slow yourself down. Even if it speeds the bike up slightly
it will slow you down, which is more important.

High Jinks and Low Jinks

Most of the techniques covered so far have been those which you
are likely to need or use when you are riding in a straight line. But
as you may already have guessed, riding mountain bikes requires
more twisting and turning than riding the average road bike, so it
would make sense to have a look at the best ways to turn corners.

The natural assumption is to use the same techniques as a road
bike, that is, leaning into a turn and keeping your body tight into
and in line with the lean of the bike. This holds true on firm,
predictable surfaces but not on the majority of mountain bike tracks
off-road.

There are two basic methods of cornering on a mountain bike
and they differ only in that they are used at different speeds. Firstly,
high speed cornering. If you are going fast on a mountain bike it is
reasonable to assume that you have a good idea of what is coming
up next. Otherwise you should not be going fast. So when you come
up to a corner you can set yourself up by standing on the pedals
and leaning off the bike on the inside of the turn. Keep your weight
on the inside of the turn, and lean the bike as much as you dare
whilst keeping your body upright. If you want to, and if the surface
is good for it, you can lock up the back wheel and watch the back
of the bike overtake the front.

The advantage of hanging inside the turn is that you can jump
off without being out of control if things get too exciting, and, if
you want to, you can stab at the ground with your foot to give that
extra and sometimes vital edge of stability.

When you want to stop turning, let go of the back brake, straighten
up and get ready for the next skid turn. This style of riding is very
exciting, not particularly dangerous and great on long downhills.

Woodland is great for exploration – as long as you keep your eyes on the track.

Just make sure that there are not too many walkers or horse-riders around at the time though, as taking avoiding action is not easy when you are travelling sideways.

If you are not riding particularly fast but have some tricky corners to negotiate, such as between close-growing trees, then you can probably think of more suitable methods than locking up your back brake at regular intervals. You will still need to keep your body weight in the right place though, between the wheel axles. As you are travelling slowly, you cannot rely on centripetal force to keep you in contact with your bike as in the skid turn. You will need to use good old gravitational attraction.

You do this by leaning out of the turn, not into it. If you have to turn sharp to the left, you turn and lean the bike left but lean your body to the right. This keeps your weight over the centre line between the wheels, and stops you falling into the turn. Naturally, you will have to stand up on the pedals to do this.

If you are unlucky and find that despite leaning the other way you are still falling into the turn, you can apply a twitch of front brake. This will tend to push the bike upright, getting you nearer to a state of equilibrium. Eventually, you will be able to turn in incredibly tight circles, using the outward lean, front brake, low gear and standing-up combination. It must be better than running into a tree!

Front Wheel Techniques

One situation you will probably come up against – literally – is crunching your front wheel into a concave or convex obstacle. More simply put, a hole or a lump. This can be a ditch, rabbit-hole, tree stump, boulder or whatever. In any event, if you don't get your front wheel over it, it will throw you off without providing a full description of its physical characteristics.

The theory is that if you can lift your front wheel over the problem, it should get to the other side of the lump/dip before you lose control. If the front wheel can be plonked down on the other side, and as long as you keep pedalling, you should be able to keep riding, albeit bumpily.

So how do you get the front wheel to lift itself obligingly over the woodpile? You do a wheelie. To wheelie, you need to be in a fairly low gear, and preferably going in a straight line. Lean forward over the bars, then simultaneously straighten up, pull on the bars and pedal hard. The joint effect of you moving your weight up and back, pulling on the bars and applying extra torque at the rear wheel will make the front wheel lift off the ground. As long as you do them all together.

Having lifted the front wheel, don't panic and throw your weight forward over the bars again. If you do, the front wheel will smack down on to the dirt, jarring your arms and spoiling your style. Try to keep the front wheel light, if not actually airborne, as long as you can. Keeping the pressure on the pedals and your weight well back will help. A note of caution here: if you overdo it, you will throw yourself off the back of the bike. If you think this is happening, grab the back brake, and the front wheel will immediately drop back down to earth.

Having mastered the trick of lifting the front wheel, you need to get your timing right when dealing with real logs, ditches and kerbstones. If you don't you will probably drop the front wheel right into the middle of the obstacle with predictable results. You should lift the front wheel as late as possible and keep it in the air as short a time as possible. That way you are out of contact with stabilising Mother Earth for the minimum interval.

Once the front wheel is on clear ground, you will have to shift your weight forward over the bars. This lets the back wheel hop over or through the bump or lump without too much effort on your part. You will need to pedal steadily, but if you do manage to keep aboard the bike while the front wheel does its wheelie, you should find the back wheel will simply follow like a faithful pet. Remind yourself that practice makes perfect if you can't manage it first, or indeed second time.

Steps and Jumps

The wheelie/lean-forward technique will take you up steps too. If you can keep the front wheel light, and the pedals turning, then you can climb up as many as three or four steps at a time. If you are a brute, you can go up more than that by smashing into the bottom steps and letting your speed carry you up as far as it can. Tyre pressure is important here. Too low a pressure and your weight will squash the tyre and tube between the step and the rim, and you will get an instant and explosive flat. This will ruin tube, tyre and probably rim too. Even if the tyre pressure is high enough to withstand an immediate puncture, you will still demolish rims and tyres at an alarming rate using this method. So think twice unless you are a bike shop owner.

Going down steps is easy once you have convinced yourself that a flight of steps is no more than a steep, very bumpy slope. The greatest barrier is almost always psychological, not physical. As long as you keep your weight well off the back of the saddle, knees bent to absorb the bumps, and leave the front brake alone, you can ride down some fearsome-looking flights. Two things make it easier. Firstly, don't go too slow, or the front wheel is likely to twist itself from your grip as the bike bumps down each step. Secondly, start from some distance before the steps start; that way you will be nicely stable when you begin bumping, and you will also get less of a chance to bottle out. If you do try to stop half-way down it can be

Riding down steps is a careful balance of control, stance and nerve, but you may prefer to watch.

Discretion is the better part of valour.

Opposite *Keeping your body weight back to ensure that the rear wheel lands first is essential when jumping. A high-speed jump is generally easier to control than a slow-speed one.*

very difficult to put your feet on solid ground without damaging yourself.

Jumps on a mountain bike are fun. Once you have perfected wheelies, all you have to do is lift the back wheel as well, and you are in business. Or in this case, in the air.

You can either use the ground contours to help, or rely on leg power. If you have a local area which features miniature versions of the Val d'Isere ski jump, then all you need do is ride hard at the jump, lift the front wheel as you take off, and make sure you land rear wheel first with your legs bent. If you land on the front wheel, you will find that it is *very* difficult to steer. If you don't have your

legs slightly bent to absorb the landing shock, you may jar yourself
severely. Try small jumps at first, then, as your courage builds,
extend your flights. Jumps of nearly 20 ft have been made by some
riders.

If you live in the Fens or on a beach, you will have to use leg
power to get you above ground level. You will not be leaping 20 ft,
but you can certainly try. Start off by using the same technique as
the wheelie, but as the front wheel comes up in the air, push back
against the pedals with both feet. At the same time, crook your legs
suddenly – a sort of kneeling action. If you have pushed back with
your feet sufficiently hard for your shoes to grip, you will find that
instead of you dropping down on to the bike, it comes up to you,
the back wheel rising in the process. If you pull your weight up
centrally, rather than back as for the wheelie, it will help both
wheels to lift together. And, as with the first jump technique, make
sure your back wheel touches first or else. . . .

The different hints, tips and ideas suggested in this chapter will
help you get more fun from your mountain bike, but, as with all
sports, there is no substitute for practice. It is always more
interesting to try to improve your style with at least one or more
like-minded biker. Imagine plonking head first into a rabbit-hole
with no one to laugh at your predicament. How boring it would be
if no one was there to witness your first wheelie.

Share your new skills and old failures, take it easy with body and
bike and you will find yourself not only hooked, but a crusading
missionary in search of old dogs to teach new tricks. See you out
there soon.

4 Where to Ride your Mountain Bike

The bicycle has always been a vehicle on which to escape to the great outdoors and cyclists were a strong force during the open air movement earlier this century. Bicycles are undoubtedly at home in the country – there is less traffic, less pollution and less noise. However, there is still a widely held view that the bicycle's place is on, rather than off, the road.

Thin-tyred racing bikes and stout touring cycles demand a smooth surface to insulate them from rough and dirty, earth tracks. The riders of these speed machines are content to whizz along black, tarmacked ribbons, soaking up the countryside through their ears, eyes and noses. Mountain bikers, however, like to get a little closer to reality. They like to leave the security of the seductive corniche, and commune intimately with hedges, ditches, rocks and mud. They can even become so obsessed that they actually believe they are part of nature.

Your attitude to all things natural may be along the lines of 'Hello birdies. Hello clouds,' or it may be more hedonistic – 'Where can I find the muddiest, filthiest puddle which will cover me from head to toe?' Either way, nature is rather big and very forgiving to the lone mountain biker. The only restrictions upon you are those of the law and of politeness and consideration to others.

Responsible Riding

Mountain bikes provoke a lot of interest among non-mountain bikers. They are fascinated by the eccentricity of the activity and by the highly technical machines. So if you meet a group of butterfly collectors outside a country church, don't be surprised if they engage you in conversation and marvel at your madness. You in turn may express wonderment at their hobby.

On the whole, you will find that people you meet in the country are tolerant of your obsession and will even go out of their way to help you achieve your destination. They will recognise in you a kindred spirit and will be pleased to make your acquaintance. In turn, you will feel well-disposed towards them and will be your charming, good-natured self. Thus, mountain biker shall live in harmony with farmer, horse-rider, rambler and butterfly collector.

This blissful state of affairs can be promoted by you everywhere you ride. If you treat everyone and everything that you meet with respect and consideration, you will always be able to pass happily on your way. This may sound like preaching – it *is* preaching – but mountain biking is a latecomer to the countryside and it must abide by the traditions established by those who have prior claim. After all, being considerate is not very difficult once you get away from the traffic that terrorises you on the road.

Back in 1984 NORBA (UK), now called the Mountain Bike Club, published the *Off-Road Code*. It was an attempt to instil a sense of responsibility and good conduct in its members and to stop clashes similar to those that had occurred in the US between mountain bikers and ramblers. The code is quite simple and has, so far, achieved its aims. This success will only continue if mountain bikers continue to follow it, accepting it in the spirit in which it was written, that is, one of advice rather than instruction.

THE OFF-ROAD CODE

- Only ride where you know you have a legal right.
- Always yield to horses and to pedestrians.
- Avoid animals and crops. In some circumstances this may not be possible, at which times contact should be kept to a minimum.
- Take all litter with you.
- Leave all gates as found.
- Keep the noise down.
- Don't get annoyed with anyone, it never solves any problems.
- Always try to be self-sufficient, for you and your bike.
- Never create a fire hazard.

- Avoid bunching up with other riders and obstructing a trail.
- Always tell someone where you are going and give an estimated time of arrival.
- Smile a lot.

You should also follow the *Countryside Access Charter* which is published by the Countryside Commission.

EXCERPTS FROM THE COUNTRYSIDE ACCESS CHARTER

- You can ride on bridleways, which are sometimes waymarked in blue.
- You can ride on byways, which are sometimes waymarked in red.
- Landowners can require you to leave land to which you have no right of access.
- Help keep all water clean.
- Protect wildlife, plants and trees.
- Take special care on country roads.
- Keep to public paths across farmland.

When riding in woodland you should observe the Forestry Commission's guidelines.

EXCERPTS FROM THE FOREST CODE

- Leave things as you find them. Take nothing away.
- Do not leave open or obstruct gates and, for your own safety, keep clear of forestry operations. Respect the work of the forest.
- Camp only on approved land.
- Obtain permits when required.
- Respect the peace and quiet of the forest and avoid disturbing others.

By bearing all three sets of guidelines in mind and by riding with common sense you are guaranteed to have a good time on the range and you will have done your bit to further the progress of mountain biking.

Legal Rights of Way

It is all very well knowing how to behave on the range, but if you don't know *where* you can ride legally you could end up setting the cause back by ten years. Trespassing and conspiracy to trespass are not nice accusations to have thrown in your face by a justifiably angry landowner. Much of the country is part of the agricultural and forestry industries and the businessmen who own it do not necessarily welcome uninvited and potentially expensive intruders. No matter how romantic you get about the country, the fact is that landowners and landworkers make their living from it. If you threaten their living they will threaten you.

The law in England and Wales is different from that in Scotland, so each will be dealt with separately, but there is one common factor – if you get permission from the landowner to ride on his land then you are laughing. Getting permission from landowners or their tenants is not necessarily very difficult. They too are human and may well have the same attitude as the butterfly collectors. You should, of course, present yourself as responsible, considerate and mindful of their concerns. You would do well to point out that mountain bike tyres are nowhere near as damaging as horse or cow hooves. It may also be prudent to explain that you follow the *Off-Road Code* and that a mountain bike is not a motorbike. They may even be interested in taking a look at your machine. Mind you, the landowner or tenant will probably not have the time to go into details, so be clear, quick and polite. When they say yes and you get to ride that cliff path which has so far been out of bounds you must keep your promises and respect any special requests.

If you cannot trace a landowner you must stick to the rights of way which are enshrined in civil law. Some routes across Ministry of Defence land are covered by criminal law which means that the penalties can be much more severe. Firstly, let's deal with the situation in England and Wales.

There are three types of off-road path which are open to mountain bikes everywhere in England and Wales: bridleways, roads used as public paths (RUPPs) and byways open to all traffic (BOATs). Unless local bylaws permit, you can only take a mountain bike on a public footpath if you carry it. Footpaths are for pedestrians, prams and dogs only. And do not think that land owned by the National Trust is a free range, it is not. The Trust may allow some cycling along some of its 'discretionary bridleways' but otherwise you must stick to statutory bridleways, RUPPs and BOATs. The position is the same with the Forestry Commission, though members of the Mountain Bike Club have gained access, on a trial basis, to all the gravel paths in the New Forest. Land in the National Parks is owned by farmers and others, not by the nation, so again you must stick to the key three rights of way. The rights to use common land are owned by specific commoners, not by you, and it is they who will decide if bicycles are to be allowed across it. River beds are owned by the same people who own the river banks so 'stream-riding' is out unless you have permission. If you can get permission from any landowner to cycle across his land then all well and good. If not, you must stick to bridleways, RUPPs, BOATs and the occasional path permitted by local bylaws. Every time.

Helpful Maps

It is easy to find rights of way in your area. Indeed, you may have seen roadside signs pointing to bridleways. Otherwise, the best place to start your route-planning is an Ordnance Survey map. For a general view of the region the pink Landranger series of maps, at a scale of 1:50,000, will do the job. The neat thing about the Landranger series is that it shows at a glance likely areas for exploration. The gaps among conurbations are exposed. Woodland is obvious because it is green. The rights of way are marked in red. The Landranger maps also show roads and railway stations so that you can plan how you are going to get to and from the start of the route. And for mountain bikers who plan to stay away from civilisation for a few days the maps show the location of youth hostels and a few campsites.

Once you have located a suitable area, get hold of a green Ordnance Survey Pathfinder map, which enlarges the scale up to 1:25,000. The bigger scale shows a lot more detail and is much more useful when you are in the middle of nowhere with nothing but a cream egg to keep you going till tea-time. The Pathfinder maps show bridleways, RUPPs and BOATs as green dotted and ticked lines. They show them in some detail, illustrating where they double back, where they curve along a river's edge and even which side of a hedge they run. The maps also show contours, field boundaries, chimneys, electricity transmission lines, church towers and spires, and dozens of features which assist navigation in strange territory. If you want to know where you are going, and where you have been, use a Pathfinder map.

The problem with Ordnance Survey maps is that they are only

up to date when they are printed – the date is printed on them. It
may be two or three years since a particular Landranger map was
revised and the more detailed Pathfinders may be based on
information obtained more than ten years ago. In the main this does
not cause too much of a problem, the wholesale deletion of public
rights of way has been stemmed by country pressure groups and so
changes are no longer as huge as they once were. But in areas of
urban expansion, around new towns, major road building, and new
military ranges, Ordnance Survey maps cannot be relied upon.
Unless you know that the tracks are legal rights of way, you should
check them with your area Definitive Map.

The Definitive Maps are held by the agents of highways and
planning authorities, in other words by the County Councils in
England and Wales and the Regions in Scotland. There may also
be copies at the headquarters of local district councils. The
Definitive Maps are a wonder to behold and everyone has a right to
see them on request. They have to be kept at least on a scale of
1:25,000, but sometimes they are on the huge scale of 1:2,500, ten
times as detailed as the Pathfinder maps, showing every kink in
every path. More importantly, they show exactly every single legal
right of way and they are the legal record of all thoroughfares. If
you have checked out your route on a Definitive Map you can be
sure you are staying on the right side of the law.

If you go as far as consulting the Definitive Map you may discover
a few interesting features. For a start, what appears as a bridleway
on the Ordnance Survey map may turn out to have been dismantled
a few years ago or diverted around the other side of a new building.
Mark all the changes on your Pathfinder map so that you follow the
new line when you hit the trail. It is also possible to find the
occasional new bridleway which is not printed on the Pathfinder
map. And you may find a few routes which you have always thought
to be owned privately but which turn out to be old overgrown roads,
once maintained by the public authority but since fallen into decay.
These ruined lanes may still be owned by the public authority and
still classified as full-blown roads so you are free to ride them.
Occasionally you will come across lanes which have no known owner.
In principle you should not ride these routes and if you are
challenged by anyone you should make your apologies and your
departure. However, in practice they are quite ridable and many
have been informally adopted by the local people. The Definitive

Map will get you off the beaten track and keep you on the straight
and narrow so check it out.

Trespassers Will....

Incidentally, you can only use a bridleway, RUPP or BOAT for its
intended purpose, as a thoroughfare. When it crosses private land
you should not stray from it, nor should you park up, have a picnic
or put on a fireworks display. In fact, in the eyes of the law, you
should only use these paths to get from one place to another; you
should not stop at all as to do so would be trespassing. When you
are out on your bike and you get a puncture on a bridleway you
have no legal right to stay there and fix it. It is highly unlikely that
anyone will challenge you in such a situation, but should they do so
you must move on.

If the legal right of way which you are following is obstructed,
you can attempt to clear a path just big enough for you and your
bike with anything that is to hand, taking care not to damage the
property of innocent parties. This means that if you come across a
fallen tree you can shift it out of your way. If it cannot be moved
then you have the right to take a short diversion across neighbouring
land, again taking care not to cause damage. You are not allowed to
return to the location with equipment to destroy the obstruction,
that is the prerogative of the local highways authority. You can
inform them of the location and nature of the obstruction and
request that it be removed. They will either ask the landowner to
carry out the remedy or they will do it themselves and sometimes
recover costs from the landowner. Most likely, unfortunately, they
will not do anything until you have badgered them for weeks. In
these cases it is worth enlisting the advice and help of the local
branch of the Ramblers' Association, the Trail Riders Fellowship,
the Cyclists' Touring Club, the Byways and Bridleways Trust and
the Mountain Bike Club. An uncleared obstruction could eventually
lead to the dismantling of the path, to everyone's loss.

Now you know your rights on paths in England and Wales, you
will have no excuse to trespass. Trespassing is a civil offence and
is usually dealt with on the spot by an angry landowner using a lot
of uncivil words. Should it go to court (it rarely does), you could
be fined. Either way, the damage done to mountain biking would
be severe and could even lead to it being banned from some areas.

Conspiracy to trespass is even worse in the eyes of the law, it is a criminal offence and can be punished with a prison sentence. It is quite easy to conspire to trespass. All you have to do is say to your fellow mud-plugger, 'Let's nip across Baron Nasty's field,' and the crime has been committed. Should Baron Nasty catch you and should he prove that you have discussed crossing his field then you could be in real trouble. Conspiracy to trespass is an extremely rare charge and it is better to keep it that way.

In Scotland there is a much more civilised, yet unclear, attitude to access. It appears that, following a judgment in 1930, mountain bikers have the right to ride on all rights of way, making no distinction between footpaths and bridleways. Once again you should take care to leave no damage. In agricultural areas mountain bikers should not go haring off across crops but should keep to the locally recognised paths. All fencing, walling and hedging should be respected, as should all forms of fauna and flora. What may look like a clump of weeds could be the last colony of an ancient plant, so take no chances wherever you ride; nature got there before you and is willing to share as long as you ride carefully.

In some areas of Scotland there are the ruins of industrial activity where quarries and mines once operated. Apart from the dangers posed by derelict shafts these sites can offer great mountain biking to novices and experts alike. The old cuttings and levels built originally for horse-drawn carts or railway engines provide easy routes for climbing hillsides. The remains of the workings themselves, perhaps crater-like holes or giant spoilheaps, are the perfect facilities for riders who want to test their own bravery and bike-handling skills. No matter where you ride always take a good look at the terrain before you plunge in.

Second-hand Roads

Newcomers to mountain biking and riders who live in large conurbations often discover what seem to be perfect routes for easy riding away from the traffic: canal towpaths and the courses of old railway lines. They are extremely tempting for several reasons. Firstly, they are isolated from the roads and there is no chance that you will get knocked off by a juggernaut as you pedal along. Secondly, the cuttings and embankments have not been manicured or shuttered with concrete so there are pleasing displays of greenery. Thirdly, the towpaths and permanent ways have a surface which is comfortable to ride while providing the occasional obstacle for stimulation, such as a railway sleeper or a set of locks. Fourthly, they are pretty well flat with no steep gradients to challenge weary legs. Finally, in towns and cities they offer a completely different view – you can get to see the world which exists behind the glossy shopfronts.

The problem with these second-hand roads is that generally they are out of bounds. Do mountain bikers allow mere rules and regulations to bind them? Of course they do. Mountain biking is not about causing hassle and aggravation, it is about having a good time within the confines of the law. So, if a railway company decides to prevent anyone using the bed of an old railway track as a thoroughfare, then that is its business. On a more optimistic note, there are now dozens, if not hundreds, of miles where trains once ran and where pedestrians and cyclists can roam freely. Enlightened railway and planning authorities have realised that a redundant railway line can still serve the populace as a footpath and cycle-route. Hence Avon, Shropshire, Derbyshire and Lothian, among many others, now boast terrific off-road routes.

Canal towpaths, which are private property, are a different case entirely because they are already part of the leisure industry. The British Waterways Boards for England and Wales, and for Scotland, and three dozen private canal companies, receive income by selling boating and fishing licences. Boat owners and fishermen have been around a lot longer than mountain bikers and there are many more of them than of us, so, obviously, they get priority. But there is a way round.

The British Waterways Boards do issue permits to cyclists to allow them to pedal along the towpaths without hindrance. Although some people have reported that these licences are difficult to obtain we have had no problems, as long as our requests have been for safe and sensible routes. They state that permits will be granted where 'the requirement is justifiable, such as for journeys to work and residential access over specified lengths'.

Unfortunately you cannot get a permit which covers all the Boards' canals. You have to specify your intended route, frequency and reason for travelling it and send in a negligible fee. You then get an annual permit which must be carried with you whenever you ride the towpath. It must be produced on demand by a Board official though we have never encountered such a demand.

The British Waterways Board has recently indicated that it is willing to open up towpaths to cyclists on a wider basis, and test projects will be set up on suitable sections of the Birmingham Navigation. If you want to be legal in other areas and to fill in a few forms the headquarters of the British Waterways Board (England and Wales) is at Melbury House, Melbury Terrace, London NW1 (telephone: 01–262 6711). They can tell you which Area Leisure Officer in which region you require. The present telephone numbers are as follows:

London and the South-east	0923–31363
Gloucestershire	0452–25524
Birmingham	021–454 7091
Nottinghamshire	0602–862411
Northwich (Cheshire)	0606–74321
Castleford (W. Yorks)	0977–554351
Wigan (Lancs)	0942–323895

The British Waterways Board (Scotland) is in Glasgow on 041–332 6936. For the east of England contact Anglian Water Authority on 0480–56181. For the River Avon between Stratford and Tewkesbury ring 0386–552517 and 021–454 0473. For other waterways contact the British Waterways Board for the relevant numbers and addresses.

So, knowing your rights and your routes, you are now well equipped to hit the trail.

5 Maintaining your Mountain Bike

This is the chapter that will help point you in the right direction when it comes to maintenance, fault diagnosis and overhauling broken components. It does not pretend to be the ultimate mechanic's bible, it is more of a guidebook than a reference atlas. The idea that whatever man has made, man can adjust, improve and keep running is a very common notion; but with the increased sophistication of manufacturing techniques, materials and designs, the good old-fashioned idea that you could strip down a bike at the edge of the road with only a stone and a nail is virtually obsolete.

Given a few pointers in the right direction, however, and using the right tools for the job with the right attitude of mind, you can generally keep your off-road rocket in a good state of order. You will be able to keep at bay most of the niggling little faults which can detract from your riding pleasure. You will be able to ride at the peak of your bike/rider efficiency graph. Cannily, you will be able to point out to amazed friends why their gears keep jumping and yours don't. Or, if you like, you will just be able to watch your local cycle shop doing a complete service on your bike and understand what is going on.

Mental Attitude

Lots of people are intimidated by what the media, often inaccurately, call 'technology'. The general idea is that if anything – usually the

63

latest consumer item, and that includes mountain bikes – is given the 'high-tech' tag, then it must be slick and easy to use. It also needs, by definition, a high technologist to fix it if anything goes wrong.

Although mountain bikes are at the top of the tree when it comes to human-powered street technology, with computer designed chainrings, composite material frames and sophisticated index gearing systems, they are a bit different from the average consumer item. The bicycle has developed along a set of lines which go back a very long way – to the very early days when a stone and a nail was probably all you would find in the well-equipped cycle repair workshop. Most of the high-tech parts which give today's mountain bike its contemporary appeal are bolted or screwed on to the basic set-up that has not changed very much since 1900. That may be bad news for the technologists but it is good news for those of us with only a spanner, a stone and a nail.

Having cleared away the myth that a mountain bike is too complex, with its tens of gears, many and varied bearings and radical brake designs, for an ordinary person to be able to work on, you must convince yourself that you *can* fix it if it goes wrong. Try to adjust the bearings with a less than confident approach, and the little devils will know. They will resist your advances, split your knuckles, jump out of their places and hide under the sink.

Your ability will rise in line with your confidence. There is *nothing* on a bike that you cannot fix, so tell yourself that before you start. Having said that, it is sometimes difficult to do it properly without the correct tools and lots of spare time. But if you do decide you are going to do a job, keep on going until you finish it. Hesitate and you are lost. Remember Tommy the Tank Engine panting 'It can be done, it can be done.' A positive mental attitude is essential for a healthy mountain bike and effectively adjusting a gear mechanism can be as enjoyable as doing your first wheelie.

Cleaning

Although not something you will normally find under 'maintenance' in other bike books, cleaning is an essential part of caring for a mountain bike. Go out for one muddy ride then leave the bike without cleaning it for a week, and it will be in a sorry state. The chain will be rusty, the gears inoperative, brakes harsh as sandpaper

The jet-wash is still the best way to get rid of the day's mud. Remember to relubricate the chain, gears and cables afterwards.

and the cables stiff as spaghetti left in the saucepan. The bike will feel as though it is ten years older.

What is the best way to clean your bike? The easy answer is to take it along to the jet-wash. High pressure water sprays as found on many large garage forecourts will clean all the mud and gunk off almost every part of the bike, including the tyres and wheels. The advantage of these water-jet cleaners is that they do not abrade the paintwork, and yet they get all the dirt out of the little nooks and crannies, even around the derailleur jockey wheels. They do leave the bike dripping wet though, and may force water into the bearings and down the cable outers.

Alternatively, you can use a bucket of water and a soft brush when the bike is still freshly dirty, or let the surface crust dry then use a stiff brush to get rid of the excess baggage. Brushing with the bike wet is not really recommended, as grit can be pushed into places where it ought not to be, such as the pedal bearings. Brushing with the bike dry will not do any harm to the bike, but does produce an instant dust cloud which can damage personal relationships if you do it indoors. Both brush methods tend to scratch the paintwork. A jet wash will keep your paint job shiny, as will dunking the bike in the nearest fast moving river. The latter method is the cheapest and most ecologically righteous, but you need to live a short road ride away from such a river.

One final word about cleaning. Your bike may still function if you never clean it, but simple maintenance tasks are made much easier if you can see what you are doing rather than working on something hidden below a layer of dust, grease and mud. Clean is easy.

Lubrication

When you have cleaned your bike down, you will need to lubricate it. If you used the jet wash all the surface coatings (and that includes oil and grease as well as the extra dirt) will have been blasted away. And possibly water will have got into the bearings.

Regarding the outside bits – chain, gears, operating cables – simply spray a new layer of moisture-displacing non-fluorocarbon-driven lube on to, or down, the relevant surface or hole. Thick sprays are not really any good if you jet wash regularly. Thin lubricant will pick up less dust and, if you keep on jetting it off

Lubricate the chain by winding the pedals backwards as you squirt aerosol lube on the links.

anyway, there is no advantage to the greater staying power of the thicker type. With regard to the bearings – hubs, bottom bracket, headset and pedals – make sure these are initially packed with waterproof grease. This will stop the water, if any does get in, mixing with and emulsifying the grease. Emulsified grease ruins the whole set-up through lack of effective lubrication whilst at the same time giving the appearance of a well-greased bearing. Emulsified grease looks milky white, a little like clotted cream. If yours looks like that, renew it pronto.

If you have got what manufacturers somewhat optimistically call 'sealed bearings', then there is little you can do to check what is going on inside. These bearings are not sealed against the ingress of nature's (or the jet wash's) bountiful gifts, they are sealed to keep the grease, or whatever lubricates them, in. So if you jet wash, or ride for any length of time with them underwater, it is a fair bet there will be water in there somewhere. However, you can only see inside by replacing the whole thing, so you are unlikely to check every time you go for a ride. The best bet is to try to keep your bike in a warm place, with it leaning slightly to one side. This will help any trapped water to evaporate or run out. Otherwise, just keep your fingers crossed, and smear waterproof grease around the spindle/seal faces.

Good old oil from a can still has its part to play in keeping the lubrication factor high. In places where a squirt of spray would not be accurate enough, or would be too thin a coating, bicycle oil can come to the rescue, for example on brake pivots. If you go squirting aerosols near the brake blocks or rim, the brakes will be efficient mechanically, but very inefficient in the frictive sense. That is to say, your brakes will not actually work. The oil can will apply just what you want, exactly where you want it. Thick oil can sometimes be used as a quick solution if a greased bearing has run dry. If you have not got the time or inclination to strip it down completely, you can just loosen the bearing or remove the cover, squirt in a few ccs of oil and tighten up before riding off.

Toolkit

Root around in every bike shed and you will find three standard tools: an adjustable spanner, a screwdriver with a rounded blade and a tyre lever. That is just about all you need to keep your mountain bike going, but a few extras are helpful at times. A good basic kit is as follows:

One good quality 6-in adjustable spanner (better than medium quality ring/open spanners, and more versatile). Just be careful that you don't round nuts off by virtue of poor adjustment though. The range of nuts the spanner should fit is from 5 mm to 15 mm, so check before you buy. Make sure it will fit front and rear wheel nuts, as these need a tough operator to loosen them sometimes. Other spanners you will need are cone spanners with very thin blades to adjust hubs, and some little ring spanners (8, 9 and 10 mm) for adjusting cable anchors in conjunction with the adjustable spanner. Special three-way box spanners are available in these sizes. If you can get hold of one of those horrid flat, stamped-out, multi-function spanners as supplied by certain large cycle manufacturers, they have slots to fit headsets and bottom bracket lockrings, so can be useful. The only other thing they are good at is making great holes in the palm of your hand while you are using them. Treat them with care. **Screwdrivers** (not with rounded blades). If they do, you will

A typical toolkit. The only special tools are a crank extractor, chainbreaker, spoke key and C-spanner. The others are Allen keys, spanners and screwdrivers.

inevitably chew up all the screw slots on your bike thus ruining them. You will need a cross slot and a Phillips head driver; some toolsets come with two blades which fit into one handle to save weight.

Allen keys, or socket head drivers. Most mountain bikes use Allen bolts on the gears, brakes, chainset, levers, bars and saddle. You would thus find it hard to manage a service without a set of Allen keys ranging in size from 4 mm to 7 mm. Penknife-style sets are available, again saving a bit of weight and the possibility of losing one down a drain. You lose them all instead!

Chain breaker or link extractor. An invaluable tool which allows you to split the chain at any link, then rejoin it again without incurring damage to the chain, your knuckles, the nail and stone.

Spoke key. For tightening loose spokes, replacing broken ones and truing buckled wheels.

Tyre levers. Trendily coloured, reinforced nylon sets of three are now available. Banish bent spoons from your kitchen drawer when you buy a set.

This simple toolkit should get you started on the road to maintaining
your own bike, but if you want to dig deeper into the world of
bearing surfaces, ratchets and pawls, and chainline adjustment, then
you will need some other special tools, like crank extractors,
freewheel removers, adjustable peg spanners. Your best bet is to
hire such specials from the local bike shop.

Where to Work on your Bike

The best place to work is somewhere clean, well-lit, warm and with
a solid floor. Running water and electricity are also useful. If that
sounds like a description of your kitchen, that is no coincidence
because the kitchen is usually the best place to do bike repairs.

Unfortunately, most mountain bikers end up in the dark, cold,
garden shed, hunting for ball bearings between the cracks in the
floor by the light of a torch. The best compromise is to hang the
bike up in the shed, remove the part you wish to work on, then sneak
it into the kitchen whilst no one is looking. Use a sheet or two of
newspaper to work on. This keeps criticism to a minimum, makes
it easier to clean up, and helps to prevent you losing tiny screws and
the like.

A tin, or plastic margarine tub (empty and washed out), is good
for keeping dismantled parts in, and can be used to rinse them in
paraffin if supercleaning is necessary. Make sure the empty tub is
polythene-, not polystyrene-based. The latter will simply melt when
you pour the paraffin in, with embarrassing results. Some odd scraps
of torn-up rag will also usually be needed to wipe excess grease and
dirt off the parts on which you are working.

Scheduled Maintenance

The best way to keep your mountain bike on the mountains is to
give it a regular once-over. Not just the BAT/HAS/WAG/PAC
which you will come across in Chapter 6, but a proper scheme of
preventive maintenance. Waiting until something breaks or goes
wrong is not a very sophisticated method of fault elimination.

Weekly maintenance
Chain: The first thing to look at is the chain. At the very least it
will need a clean and relubrication. If you don't have one of those

neat gadgets which grips the chain between rotary brushes and spins it in a bath of paraffin as you turn the pedals backwards, then clean it with a rag soaked in spray lubricant. Any stiff links or projecting pins should be rectified using the chain breaker. Any tendency for the chain to ride up on chainring or sprocket teeth indicates wear, either on chain or rings/cogs. Check amount of wear as in monthly maintenance then, when it has dried off, lubricate with whatever you usually use.

Wheels: Next give the wheels a once over; tyres first. Apart from the obvious (a flat), check for thorns sticking out, correct seating on the rims and no sidewall damage. The last mentioned can cause quite dramatic blow-outs. Replace the tyre if it is at all suspect. If the rims are out of true, or dented, then it is time to dig out the spoke key. Resting a fat felt-tip pen on one brake block, spin the wheel, so that the pen leaves a mark on the side of the rim at the points of greatest wobble. Then tighten the spoke nearest the mark which goes to the other side of the hub. Do this by turning the nipple (square brass thing which fits into the rim) a mere quarter of a turn at a time, like a screw head. As the spoke gets tighter, it pulls the rim slightly across the hub as well as in, and so straightens

Marking a buckled rim with a marker pen prior to trueing the wheel with a spoke key.

Hub bearings take a pounding and can be tightened or slackened using cone spanners. The use of two spanners stops the axle turning during adjustment.

out the wobble. Take it very slowly, one spoke at a time until the wheel looks better. If it looks worse, think positive and try again, making sure you use a new set of felt-tip pen marks.

If you have ridden up kerbs a lot you will probably have flats on the rim where the lips which grip the tyre have bent outwards. Using a vice if you have one, or Mole grips if you don't, squeeze the two bent sections of rim back together to the original profile. More serious flats will probably need a new rim.

Wheel hubs will need to be checked for correct running. If there is any sideways movement at all in the hub, or if the wheel is reluctant to turn, remove the wheel. Then the bearing locknuts will need loosening and the bearings adjusting. Do this by screwing the adjusting cones in or out with the cone spanner. Once the wheel spins smoothly again, retighten the locknuts and refit the wheel. Make sure you fully tighten the wheel nuts or quick-release so that the wheel stays in next time you ride the bike.

Brakes: Weekly brake inspections can be limited to making sure that the brake blocks have not worn down too much, that they sit

If U-brakes are not properly centred relative to the rim some can be adjusted with a neat little screw which alters spring tension. This ensures the brakes never rub.

squarely on the rim, and that both sides pull away when you release the lever. If the blocks are not parallel to the rim, you risk scoring the rim metal when they wear down to support level. Use your Allen keys and small ring spanners to make sure all the blocks are on line, and bearing centrally on the rim walls. If one block seems to rub all the time, it could be either a weak spring, or more simply the straddle wire (the wire that connects the two sides of the brake together) being offset. Check it before you start adjusting spring pressures. Many brakes now have adjusters built in to compensate for spring pressure. If yours don't, remove the straddle wire and pull the brake block as far away from the rim as you can against the force of the spring. This should bend the spring slightly and give more equal return pressure on both sides.

Check the cables are not fraying anywhere – especially where they come out of the brake levers. Frayed cables will often cause stiff operation and rubbing blocks. If any cables look at all doubtful, renew them immediately. If one breaks when you brake, then you break too. Check the brake-lever fit on the bars, and the lever pivot bolt. These sometimes vibrate loose and drop out. Outer cables should be oiled as a matter of course; use a squirt can or aerosol with a tube instead of a spray to lubricate down into the cables. Bare cables deserve a wipe over to stop them rusting. Hub brakes do not need as much attention as rim brakes, just check the cables and lever movement. Shoes will probably need replacement only about every six months even with heavy usage. And lastly, adjust the lever end cable adjusters so that the brakes lock at your preferred lever position.

Gears: Gears need looking at less often than most riders would like to think. Unless they have been bashed, or you have changed the wheel or freewheel set-up, they don't need much weekly attention.

On the rear gear, make sure the two jockey wheels which guide the chain are in line with the freewheel cogs, both horizontally and vertically. A small knock on a tree can put them out of line, making gear changing difficult and leading to excess chain and gear mechanism wear. If they are out of line, unscrew the whole gear mechanism from the gear hanger using a 6 mm Allen key. The gear hanger is the bit fixed to the dropout, from which the gear hangs.

If the rear gear hanger gets bent, straighten it using a spanner after having removed the gear mechanism.

Setting the stops on the rear gear mechanism will prevent the chain jamming in the spokes or the drop-out. On the end of the cable is an adjuster for fine-tuning the shifting action. Indexed gears require this to be set very accurately.

Then twist the hanger with your adjustable spanner until it is back in line, refit the gear mechanism and there you are, no more crunchy gears. You will probably need to reset the stop screws on the body of the changer so that the chain does not drop either inside or outside the freewheel, but that should be covered in the bike's instruction manual. Do that anyway if the chain keeps dropping off into the spokes or frame.

Check the jockey wheels for easy running without excess play. Lubricate or replace if necessary. Make sure the front changer is parallel with the chainrings, and correctly adjusted for outer and inner rings. Too big a vertical gap between the changer plate and the teeth of the rings can promote slow changes and worn teeth. The gap should be only around 4 mm. All cable runs should be rustless, smooth and lubricated; cable fraying should again be looked for. Adjust the cables so that there is no play in them when unstretched, especially on indexed systems. Gear lever mounts should be given a squirt of lube and tightened on the bars.

The front gear mechanism will need re-setting at intervals as the cable stretches. It is a simple job with a screwdriver. Note that the cable end has been capped. Bare cable ends can stab you in the leg.

Cranks: These can drop off if you don't tighten them now and again. Make sure the retaining bolt is tight. If there is any play, or possibly a regular clicking noise coming from the cranks, then the bolt is probably slightly loose. If it is, undo it completely and remove the crank with a screw-in crank extractor or one key release set, then put it back on at 90 degrees to its original position. This can help to avoid the opening out of the square taper on a loose crank. At the other end of the crank, make sure the pedal axle is tight home in the crank. If this is loose, it can suddenly tear out when you stand up on the pedals, with disastrous consequences. Just note that the left-hand pedal has a left-hand thread, so don't try to tighten it clockwise.

Pedals: While you are grovelling around on that bit of the bike, check out the pedals themselves. These are one of the most abused components, yet they usually get very little attention. The dust cap on the outer end should be intact and in place. Replace, if required, by levering it out with a screwdriver then pressing a new one back

The removal of both cranks can be achieved using the same tool – a crank extractor. Make sure it is screwed home before tightening the extractor bolt. If not, the threads inside the crank arm can strip.

in. A quick blob or two of grease or oil will do no harm either. The pedal should be free-running yet with no play. Any clicks or squeaks or jerky running indicate adjustment and/or lubrication is required. Adjustment is similar to the wheel hubs. With the dust cap removed, undo the outermost locknut, adjust the bearing nut, then lock up the locknut again. If your toolkit does not include the correct size box spanners, jam a screwdriver down the side of the bearing nut to stop it moving whilst you tighten the locknut on to it.

At the other end of the pedal, wipe a smear of grease around the seal between the axle and pedal body. That will help keep out water, dust and suchlike better than a dry seal.

Chainrings and Freewheel: The toothed bits on your bike are what keep you moving when you pedal. Make sure they are all present and are not likely to drop off. Some freewheels use a shallow helix spline system to stop the whole lot turning, with a small lockring to stop them coming off when you pedal backwards. Unfortunately, the lockring comes loose. If you have one like that, check it is tight on a weekly basis. The freewheel sprockets and the gaps between them should be clear of grass, twigs and rubbish. A build-up of debris does not look of any consequence, but can make the chain jump over the teeth. Cracked or broken teeth signal a visit to the bike shop for a new freewheel or, if you are brave, a new sprocket.

To lubricate the freewheel, lay the bike on its side and pour a little light oil into the open end of the freewheel. At the front end of the transmission check that all teeth are present. Bent ones on alloy chainrings can be straightened by using a pair of pliers, carefully. The five bolts and captive nuts which lock the chainrings to the crank spider should be very tight. Any looseness will spread and they will all eventually drop out, wrecking the rings. If the rings themselves are slightly bent, judicious levering with a long bar is called for. Never use a hammer, as the shocks are likely to ruin the bottom bracket bearings.

Monthly maintenance

When you buy a mountain bike, be prepared to spend more on consumables than you would for an ordinary road bike. Chains, tyres and gear mechanisms all wear more quickly off road than on. Although you should not be renewing all these components on a monthly basis, you will need to start looking closely at them at each full moon to ensure your continued off-road activity.

Chain: The chain needs to be given the same once-over as in the weekly section, but also has to undergo the stretch test. As the links wear, so the amount of slack in each link increases. This, if you leave the chain on, will wear the teeth on the freewheel and chainrings into a hook shape. As it is cheaper to replace a chain than a complete transmission system, check the chain. Shift the chain on to the large chainring, then grip the link nearest the front wheel spindle (right at the front of the chainring) and pull it forwards. If the chain is worn enough to let the link come away from the teeth on which it should be sitting, then it is due for the scrap-heap. More than 5 mm of radial movement should condemn it. Use the chain breaker to remove it, clean all toothed bits and fit the new one. Make sure you fit exactly the same number of links as the one you took off – you will have gear-change problems if you don't.

Wheels: Test the spokes every month, not just by spinning the wheel to check for trueness. Spin the wheel, and lightly ping each spoke with a small screwdriver as they race past. Any oddly tensioned spokes will show themselves by an unusually high or low note. Re-tension any with the spoke key, then retrue the wheel as per weekly maintenance. When you have done that, remove the tyre, tube and rim tape. Look all around the inside of the rim for any spoke ends which your retruing may have poked through into the well of the rim. If you leave any spoke ends protruding, they will puncture your inner tube from the inside and leave you fuming. File ends down or clip them off. As you replace the tyre and tube, run your hand round the inside of the tyre to locate and remove any small thorns which may be working their way into your inner rubber. Check the tube for folds and pinched sections, and make sure the valve/tube join is sound. Running at low pressures can cause splits there.

The hubs should not yet need regreasing, so check the adjustment as per weekly schedules, but also look for bent axles. Hold the wheel still, and spin the axle from one end. Any out-of-true will show itself instantly. If the axle is bent, replace it. Check none of the bearings has been damaged by whatever caused the axle to bend. Also make sure that the dropouts are parallel to each other – this is a common cause of bent axles. Rectify, if necessary, with the adjustable spanner.

Brakes: Undo the brake pivot nuts or bolts, take off the actual brake arms themselves and clean and lubricate the mounting studs. Reassemble the arms and reset the spring pressure on each as described in 'weekly maintenance'. Take the cable inners out of the outers, clean and relubricate them and refit. Check the ends of the outers; the coils which make up the flexible sheath sometimes lose shape and overlap or kink. If any are like this, clip them off as they promote inner cable fraying. Check the nipples which are located in the brake lever itself. They sometimes pull off, so any signs of movement indicate they need immediate replacement. Lubricate inside the outers, re-thread and refit, making sure the lever end adjusters have their maximum adjustment available.

Hub brakes should be taken apart, and checked for grease seeping into the drum. If there is any, replace the shoes. Some people try baking them in a hot oven. This may or may not get them frictional again, but will certainly serve to annoy the cook in any household.

Loose dust and debris should be cleaned out, and the pivot pins very lightly lubricated with high temperature grease.

Gears: These need to be taken off the bike every month and given a thorough cleaning. Dunk them in a paraffin bath, scrub their every cranny with a redundant toothbrush and give them a complete new coat of light spray lube when they are dry. Front changers may need their cages to be bent back in slightly if they have had any smash-ups on the trail. Rear changers need their jockey wheels stripped. Swap top and bottom jockey wheels to even up wear. Check the spring tension in the parallelogram as well as top and bottom pivots. Some gears have a tension adjustment facility; increasing this will usually give less likelihood of slipping, but slower changes. Make your choice now. All cables should be stripped, cleaned and relubricated. Check inners and outers for fraying, compacting and kinks, especially on index systems. Worn ferrules – the brass bits at the end of each outer – will make index systems hard to adjust, so check they are in mint condition.

Gear levers can be stripped down if they are failing to keep you in the gear you want to be. Clean all traces of oil or other lubrication off the friction washers and reassemble.

When reassembling the gear mechanisms, reset the high and low gear stops before connecting the cables. Set the rear gear body as near to horizontal as you can by adjusting the stop if there is one. Then take up all the slack in the cables as you tighten the clamp bolts. If the system is non-index, make sure all gears, both front and rear, are easy to get. For index systems, set them as follows. Try to change from top click to second click. If the chain does not move, adjust the cable tension until it just drops into second. Then increase the cable tension until the chain starts to rub on the third sprocket, then back off the adjuster by a quarter turn. You are now ready to click off.

Cranks: Take the cranks off even if they look healthy, clean the square tapers and refit them at 90 degrees with a smear of margarine on the surfaces. Do them up *tight*.

Pedals: Completely strip the pedals down each month, check their internal condition, and grease if needed. Remove them from the cranks, clean the threads and refit them with a smear of grease. If you don't do this at intervals, they tend to seize up in the cranks and sometimes strip the thread when you try to undo them. A washer between pedal spindle and crank also helps stop this happening. If you are a maniac, sharpen up the teeth on the beartraps with a file.

Bottom Bracket: The bottom bracket spindle may be slightly loose (or stiff) after a month or so. Firstly, make sure the fixed cup on the right-hand side is absolutely tight. It has a left-hand thread. Then loosen the notched lockring on the adjustable left-hand cup, and, using a peg spanner, set the cups correctly. The cranks should spin freely without slop.

Headset: No movement should be apparent in the headset, apart from a smooth turning motion. Put the front brake on, and rock the bike back and forth. Any slack will be felt as a dull clicking. If the headset is tight, with a kind of ratchet feel to its movement, it is *too* tight. Loosen the locknut on the top of all the other washers, nuts and spacers, then adjust the top adjustable cup by hand to the desired, smooth setting. Tighten up the locknut as tight as you can.

Stem and Bars: Loosen, then retighten all the stem and bar locking bolts after giving them a squirt of lube; this makes them easier to undo next time. Remove the stem by undoing the stem bolt and then tapping it firmly with a hammer down into the fork column. Lubricate the outside of the stem and inside of the fork column. This avoids the stem seizing up, a very embarrassing experience. Check-tighten the levers and their mounts, and turn the grips around if they are wearing a lot on the upper face. Use the screwdriver/water method, mentioned in Chapter 9, to loosen them, then dry them and push them back on. Don't bother with glue of any sort as it will only make a mess and is not guaranteed to solve a slippery grip problem.

Twice yearly maintenance
You will need to delve into the innermost recesses of your bike every six months or so. A complete strip-down is called for. In addition to all the obvious parts which whirr, click and collect grit on the outside, there are a few hidden areas which, although usually very reliable, will benefit from a glimpse of daylight now and again. Such parts are headsets, bottom brackets and wheel hubs. When you have removed all the bolt-on parts, you will need to check them out as follows.

The C-spanner is used to undo the bottom bracket locking ring so you can then adjust the bearings inside. Make sure the locking ring is tight – loose bearings can ruin a bottom bracket.

Bottom Bracket: Firstly, remove both cranks. Then, using a C-spanner, undo the adjustable cup lockring (right-hand side, right-hand thread). Then undo the adjustable cup itself. You may need a peg spanner, or possibly a nail and a stone, to get it loose. When it has come right out, carefully pull it and the axle out of the bottom bracket tube. Don't drop any ball bearings over the floor in the process. Next, fish around inside the other (fixed cup) side of the bottom bracket tube for the rest of the ball bearings. Clean all the balls and the surfaces on which they run with a rag, then check everything to see if any cracks or pits have developed since you last peeped inside. Any blemishes mean a new item. If one or more balls is pitted or cracked, renew the lot. Incidentally, you don't actually need to remove the fixed cup from the frame to do this. They are usually very tight so it is better not to try anyway.

Re-assemble the whole with lots of waterproof grease, and a plastic axle sleeve if you can find one. This stops dirt dropping down the seat tube into the bearings when some joker steals your saddle ten miles from home. Adjust the axle to spin without play, lock the locknut tight and speed off refreshed.

If you have a sealed-unit bottom bracket, all you can do is to check it for play, wear or stiffness. If it has any of these three, you can either try to replace the bearing cassettes or chuck it away and buy a new one. Usually the former process is such a lengthy and expensive one, involving special tools, special order from the supplier and a six-week wait, that you are better off going for a cheap plastic replacement while you wait. Sealed units usually last for about a year, if treated well, then fail catastrophically, so the spare plastic one will be a good idea anyway.

Headset: This will need cleaning down every six months to stop pitting of the races. What happens is that as you leap carelessly off four-foot drops, the little balls in the headset dig little pits in the races in the straight-ahead position (if you land with the bars in the straight-ahead position that is, and you will find landings tricky if you don't), giving rise to a ratchety feeling in the steering. You will need to remove the stem and bars, undo the locknut and drop the forks out, after unscrewing the top headset race. Doing this without the front wheel in makes things easier. Then clean and inspect the balls and bearing faces as with the bottom bracket; reject and replace dud items. Using a long rod or screwdriver with a hammer, gently tap out the bottom bearing from the head tube, turn it exactly a quarter turn and tap it back in. This will stop any pits in the races from lining up, and so allow you to leap off four-foot drops for twice as long as you otherwise could.

Re-assemble, taking care not to pinch the rubber seals, if there are any, and tighten to the requisite tension and jump.

Wheel Hubs: These are stripped down and serviced in exactly the same way as the bottom bracket, and should be subject to the same checks and re-assembly process. If they are fully sealed units, that is, cassette-bearing units rather than having simple rubber seals outside a standard cup and cone arrangement, then you cannot be quite so cavalier as with the bottom bracket. Throwing the sealed bearings away means throwing the whole wheel away too. So you will have to remove the axle, tap out the old cassettes, then press some new ones in. It is easy to ruin a hub by doing this badly, so take it to a shop if you are at all unsure.

While you are close to the hubs, check that no cracks are visible where the spokes thread through the flanges. Spokes have been known to pull right out of a hub as a result of overtightening.

Frame: When you have the complete bike stripped, you might as well give the frame a once-over for cracks, dents and bends. Likely areas for cracks are dropouts, near any joints, top of the seat stays, and the bottom of the clamp slot on the seat tube. Check frame alignment by sighting from the head tube across the seat tube to the rear axle. Any misalignment will show up without all the other components tacked on. Any frame problems should be referred to your local expert.

You can give a squirt of lube down the inside of all the tubes if you want. This will help dispel moisture and stop rust. It certainly will not do any harm anyway.

If you manage to follow this maintenance schedule, you should have the best looking, most efficient and safest mountain bike within miles.

Mobile Toolkit

Just in case you break down away from home, then here is a good idea of what to take as a toolkit for the trail.

The adjustable spanner is an essential. You will not really need any others, but one of the flat, stamped-out horrors as previously mentioned can be useful. You need slot head and cross head screwdrivers; 4, 5 and 6 mm Allen keys; a pair of tyre levers; spoke key and a chain breaker. Oh, and a pump, making sure it fits the valves you have on your tubes. A spare tube and a couple of patches plus some glue complete the kit. That lot should see you right for all but the severest breakdowns.

If you are the careful type, then a couple of spare links, a spare brake cable and few nuts and bolts will give you that extra peace of mind. But when it comes to the crunch, or rather avoiding the crunch, the best way to avoid getting stuck is to develop a feel for how your bike is working. Any noises that are out of the ordinary should be investigated. Clicks, scrunches and grinding are the precursors to a breakdown. If you ignore them, they may go away, but they may also suddenly increase in volume as the front changer tries to follow the chain around the chainset. Try to develop a feel for the inner workings of your bike, be at one with the smooth tick-tack of chain on jockey.

6 Recreation and Ride Planning

You are about to embark on a mountain biking expedition. You are all set to go. Or are you? Have you checked the tyre pressures? Have you checked the brakes? Have you got the right map? Do you have a first aid kit? Can you take your bike on the train? Are your muscles rippling? Have you told your mum where you are going?

Oh dear, the great cloud of sensible precautions is gathering on your horizon, threatening to take away the wonderful thrill of just jumping on and heading westward, ho. But of course it need not. If you are well prepared for any outdoor activity, not only is the activity itself enhanced, but slight problems are much less likely to become major disasters.

BAT/HAS/WAG/PAC

Your bike comes first. Although checklists are a bit of a bind, try BAT/HAS/WAG/PAC. More explicitly: brakes and tyres, headset and saddle, wheels and gears, pedals and chain. It might help jog your memory.

Brakes and Tyres: Check that your brakes are adjusted correctly, if the lever end adjusters are at their full extension, slacken them off and take up the cable slack at the brake caliper end. Resetting these in fading light on the top of your local mountain because you dare not trust the brakes on the descent can be tedious. Check you have enough brake block/pad material left to allow for a lot of wear. Some sandy, wet tracks can wear blocks right down in one day. If

in doubt, put a couple of spares in your bag. Make sure you cannot
see or feel any frayed lengths of cable anywhere. These spell danger.
Check your tyres are pumped up as hard as you left them. Slow
punctures sometimes turn into fast ones, for example when the valve
rips out of the tube. Some of the puncture sealant magic mixes now
available can be useful if you puncture often, but don't forget to
renew the liquid at intervals. Change dodgy tubes and check tyres
for wear, not only on the tread pattern, but where the tyre meets
the rim. Badly adjusted brakes which rub and prolonged low tyre
pressures can lead to breakdown of the tyre-casing. This causes a
blow-out when you least expect one. Remove obvious thorns, flints
and sharp objects, and check for leaks if you pull any out.

Headset and Saddle: These are two of the most common fixtures
for self-loosening on any mountain bike. Both should be correctly
adjusted and tightly locked. Loose saddles cause great personal
discomfort, and after a while become incapable of correct
adjustment. In addition, they usually develop a habit of pointing at
the sky when you land after a jump – this can be very painful.
Loose headsets wear quickly and have been known to cut through
steering columns. Headsets also, if left loose, cause opening out of
the head tube into which they are a press fit. After a while they
cease to be a press fit, and ruin an otherwise perfect frame because
no headset will fit. Both saddle and headset only take seconds to
check and adjust in the comfort of your own home.

Wheels and Gears: The wheels should be true, with no obvious
loose spokes. Hubs should not have excessive slop in them, or be
squeakily stiff. Both can cause failure of the axle or bearings. Check
wheel nuts or Q/R levels are tight. Wheelies can be terrifying if the
front wheel drops out. Gears should be smooth, able to get the
whole range without stretch or slack in the cable. Adjust the stops
and cable if necessary; loose cables catch on things, and a balking
gear is a real nuisance. Some adjustment will be needed during the
working life of any gear mechanism to allow for wear, so remember
to check. Check the chainring and freewheel for missing teeth. Any
absent or damaged ones could multiply under the stress of a fierce
hillclimb.

Pedals and Chain: Pedals include the whole chainset assembly.
Everything should be smooth and slop-free. Cranks come loose

rarely, but if you don't have the right tightening tool for the odd occasion they will simply become unusable. What happens is the square hole in them becomes rounded out by the axle, and eventually comes loose no matter how much you tighten it. One key release systems are best for avoiding this little problem. Pedals run dry, get grit in them, or both, then seize up. Bottom brackets do likewise and eat ball bearings at an alarming rate. This gives you the choice of either not riding or buying a complete new spindle, bearing, cup and seal set. Check before you ride. The chain needs a quick once-over for stiff or split links, and a squirt of lube.

The whole of the BAT/HAS/WAG/PAC check need not take more than a couple of minutes at most, including a couple of minor adjustments and a drop of lubrication here and there. But it really can make the difference between a fond memory of plashing voles on an isolated stretch of sun-kissed riverbank, and a nightmare recollection of a bruising, muddy, ten-mile trek, carrying a broken bike to the nearest village to find that there were no buses and the phone box did not work. Bet your life Baden Powell would have been a BAT/HAS/WAG/PAC man if there had been mountain bikes around in his day!

Personal Provenance

Not only does your bike need a once over before you hurtle off, so do you. If you are healthy, well equipped and well fed, you can enjoy your ride much better than if you are a poor specimen. Rather than boring you with another exotic mnemonic, we would exhort you to think ahead. Even the less food-fanatical amongst you will appreciate that a boiled egg and a cup of tea will not really be enough for a twenty-mile ride over the Black Mountains, especially if you went to a late, late party the night before.

At the risk of being too sensibly boring, a good night's sleep followed by a hearty calorie-high and protein-rich breakfast will let your stomach provide the energy you need to face the exertion of the day. Using muesli, eggs, bread, fruit and milk as fuel is better than relying on adrenalin and the depletion of muscle tissue to keep you going. Drink plenty too.

You will probably lose around four to six pints during a typical day's riding, so it is extremely easy to become dehydrated without realising it, especially if you are a newcomer to the sport, and are not yet sure how to pace yourself. Headaches and muscle pain often accompany dehydration, and will definitely spoil your enjoyment of a ride, if not ruin it completely.

It is a good idea to take some emergency rations with you when you are out on the bike, not only to stop you from becoming dehydrated, but to keep your energy levels up too. From a simple nip round the wood-block when a Mars bar will suffice, to a three-day wilderness trek when you need soup, bread, honey, beans and probably energy tablets, as well as plenty to drink. Being caught out without some extra nourishment other than the local newsagent can supply is definitely not on.

Rather than the traditional paper bags crammed with gooey sandwiches exploding out of your backpack, saddlebag and panniers, it is better to take the ingredients to make up as you want them on the trail. Don't take easily perishable foods, just staple fare. A loaf of bread, a small plastic jar of either savoury or sweet spread, and a knife will give you instant chef's delight whenever you please. Other favourites include sweetened condensed milk. Spread it on bread and revel in hedonism. Chocolate does not really do you any good, but makes you feel better for a short while. Fruit is healthy, useful and replenishes liquid levels. It may also burst in your backpack, making everything else completely unusable.

The usual energy bars and drinks must be used carefully, as they can actually be counter-productive in some instances. If you are severely dehydrated, a heavy dose of syrupy energy drink can actually worsen the situation by changing the osmotic pressure in the stomach. This can cause your vital body fluids to flow into, rather than out of, the gut. Slow release energy preparations are best, these help to reduce the risk of sugar overload and its associated energy trough. Small, frustose-based tablets are about the best and most convenient to carry and eat. Water, water and more water is essential if you are feeling a bit weak or woozy, but don't quaff huge quantities of very cold water if you are very hot. Severe stomach cramps can result.

Packing for the Trip

With respect to the actual carrying of food and drink, most people prefer either panniers or a small rucksack. The former is best to prevent you getting a sweaty back, but if you need to lift the bike much, panniers can be a real nuisance. Food tends to keep slightly better in a rucksack due mainly to the lower impact of jolts and bumps transmitted through the rider's body. Pannier stashes are best wrapped well in lots of plastic bags, with most things kept separate in case of spills and breakages. Avoid handlebar bags if you can. They have limited carrying capacity, and bounce around like crazy, mashing any food to a pulp within seconds of starting your ride.

Water should be carried in water bottles, kept in bottle cages on the frame. Most mountain bikes will have at least two bottle cage mount points, some have up to four. Fit the large one-litre bottles if you can find any, and don't leave last week's water in them. If you do, your next mouthful will taste disgusting. Some riders fit bottle cages on either side of the head tube to make the drinks easy to get at, and to keep the bottles out of the way for when they need to carry the bike on their shoulders. Wherever you decide to keep your drinks, remember to refill your water bottles at every opportunity that presents itself – you may regret it later if you don't.

This simple list of useful hints and tips on how to get ready for that 'wonderfully spontaneous' ride seems to be getting longer all the time, but after a few trips into the backwoods, you will find that all these seemingly complex preparations become second nature, and almost a part of the ride itself. Likewise, the art of dressing for the trail can seem daunting, but given a few basic pointers it is a piece of cake, or rather, cloth.

Suit Yourself

Two different sets of preferences have become evident in the recent years that have seen the rise in popularity of the mountain bike. Cyclists either dress stylishly, donning the designer/functional clothes available from their local trendy outdoor clothing and ski shop. Or they wear their most ill-assorted, old and disposable clothing. Both schools of thought have their fanatical adherents; until you have established your own loyalties here are a few pointers.

If you are the type who likes to look cool, you need the designer duds to complement your shiny new bike. Specialist gear is expensive, light, sweat and wet proof. It looks good outdoors where it tells other walkers and bikers that you are a serious operator. It is likely to be exactly what you need, keeping you at a constant temperature and humidity no matter what the outside conditions. But, if you fall off and tear anything it will break your heart and damage your bank balance. If you go for the 'wheeled hobo' look, you may be looked at askance by other people you meet in nature's playground. You will stay wet for ages if rained on, feel constricted and sweaty most of the time, thanks to the unsuitable tightness of everything, and not give a damn if you rip an entire sleeve off on a low branch or dive headfirst into a muddy pool. The choice is yours.

One thing you should always bear in mind when dressing up is that what is suitable at the start of the ride is not always the best thing on the way back. So, if you see the snow falling and don your super one-piece arctic preserver, only to discover that after six miles the sun comes out and melts the snow, you will regret it and probably melt in sympathy. The best advice, as tried and tested by the Himalayan explorers reported in Chapter 10, is to wear layers. Start off with thin thermal undies, then layer up with T-shirts, sweatshirts and waterproofs until you reach a sufficient level to keep out the very chilliest of weathers and the highest of wind-chill factors. Then if the sun comes out, all you need to do is to peel back a layer or two and bask as you ride. Thin clothes are easier to layer, and easier to stuff into luggage if you have lots of layers.

Probably most important of all is to make sure you have a windproof top to keep your torso and lower back from the super-chill effect if you get wet through. If you are soaking, either with rain or possibly sweat when you are exerting yourself, then sudden rapid cooling caused by strong wind through open clothing can cause major physiological problems. You will face a sudden loss of energy, possibly cramps and fainting too. So take a windproof top, even if it lets the water in – being wet is miserable, but being wet and cold can be dangerous.

When you have selected your wardrobe, don't forget the gloves and goggles, with a cap as well if you want head protection. All these things help to stop you being scratched, stung or whipped by branches, brambles and nettles. The goggles also help you see where you are going on long downhill swoops by stopping your eyes from watering excessively. They can make the difference between a near miss and a crash. If you are wearing baggy trousers, pull your socks over the top of them. This will stop the flapping bits catching in the chain and being shredded into tiny pieces.

For more information on clothing alternatives see Chapter 9.

Sorting the Route

Chapter 4 has given you all the information you need to get you off the beaten track without falling foul of the rules and regulations. And if you are going farther than your favourite local quarry or pub, you will probably need to take a map with you. If you are in unfamiliar territory, and have to check the map regularly, you will want to keep it somewhere handy. The best solution is a Map Flap which takes a folded OS map and holds it secure and dry, clipped on the bars. The second best answer is a clear plastic bag you can stuff down the front of your shirt. If you don't use a plastic bag to protect it, a map will soon wear through at the folds and fall to pieces. Obviously, the bag also keeps the wet out if it is raining while you are trying not to get lost. Stuffing it down the front of your shirt may sound somewhat primitive, but if you put your map into a pocket or some other easy-to-get-at place then you can be sure it will have bounced out when you went over that last particularly difficult and very wet ditch.

Ride planning is something that you will get a feel for after a while. The cryptic legends on the map become potential challenges, hinting at undiscovered secrets. Dotted lines become hedge-lined drovers' roads, stiff with the ghosts of medieval shepherds and close-packed contour lines whisper of headlong plunges to charge the bloodstream with adrenalin.

Circular routes are best; it is generally pretty boring coming back along the same track as you went out along. So look for any routes which let you go in a rough circle, passing through at least one river, one wood, two white roads and a very steep downhill, as well as close to a well-known, greasy-spoon caff. After a few forays in your chosen area, you will be surprised how many tracks and suitable routes there are which you did not even imagine, let alone the ones you knew about but had not explored. If you are near a station or possess a four-wheeler, then you can spread your net a little wider. Drive for half an hour, park the motor up, slip the bikes off the rack and away you go. Or catch a train, get off at a station which looks promising and circulate. Just check you can take bikes on the return journey though. Some local rail services have no facilities for bikes at peak hours, so you could be stranded cold and muddy on a remote station platform.

Use as many bridleways and other tracks as you can, but don't entirely avoid ordinary roads. Short stretches of main road can be quite refreshing between bouts of serious mud-plugging. The going seems so easy, you think you are doing about 45 mph and your confidence takes a hike ready for the next soggy bridleway. Look out for mud in your eyes though. The amount of dirt an ordinary tyre can hold, then flick off at even a moderate speed may surprise you. Short stretches of varied terrain are much more interesting and challenging than a long stretch of similar ground. Plan your route so that the hills work for you on the way back home when you will definitely be more worn-out than at the beginning of the ride. A massive hillclimb at the end of a twenty-mile ride is only good to make you forget all those wonderful things you have seen and done on the rest of the ride. Likewise, if the wind is blowing hard, resist the temptation to speed off with it at your back. You will only have to slog all the way back home into the teeth of the gale.

It is always useful to check the map to make sure you have a few 'get-outs' on any route. These are spots where, if you are either bent, bruised or just blown out, you can head off along relatively easy tracks or roads to nearby towns or villages. Knowing you are never more than a couple of miles from the nearest 'get-out' will give you more of a feeling of security if the weather turns nasty or if you develop a problem away from outward signs of civilisation. It is also preferable to go out with someone else if at all possible: good times and accidents are both better dealt with if there is another mountain biker to help out.

Pace-making

The way you tackle your route depends on two factors: how far you are going and how fit, or unfit, you are. If you are going out for a short bash, then you can go as hard as you want from the start. You can surge up outrageously steep hills, race for skid turns and leap ditches *ad infinitum*. You will be thoroughly wasted, soaked in sweat and happy as a sandboy, but it will not matter if you crunch the bike in your madcap pursuits because you are a mere four miles from home. This is the most publicised form of mountain biking and the easiest. Unlike other cycling pursuits, you can do it anywhere, fit or unfit, and as close to home as you feel the neighbours can cope with. But if you are unfit, or to put it more politely, less fit than you could be, beware of pushing your personal limits too far. This kind of riding exercises just about all the muscles you can think of. If any of them are a bit weak you can pull them, get cramp or simply put too much strain on them, resulting in aches for days afterwards. So until you know your limits, have a rest every few minutes to collect your breath and let the muscle tissue regroup its forces. If anyone is watching, you can pretend you are mentally preparing for the next amazing feat you are about to perform.

When riding a longer distance, it pays to get slowly into your stride as you eat up the miles. If you go as hard as you can from the start, you will find that as the ride progresses you will be spending more time staring exhaustedly down at the front wheel and wishing you were back at home by the fire. There is no fun in that, you may as well stick to doing marathons or riding 100-mile time trials. Mountain biking is about being able to stop when you like, go when you like. You will not be doing that if you have used up all your energy resources five miles back. On a longer ride, pacing is all important. Try to keep in a comfortable gear when you get to a hill. Sit down and twiddle your way up. Keep as consistent a pedal speed, or cadence, as you can. Always try to keep one gear in reserve as an ultimate fall-back. Avoid standing up on the pedals unless you have to – it is a good way to get a power burst, but expends more energy than sitting down on the saddle. To put it in a more compact fashion, ride genteelly. Elegance of style will combine with efficiency to make your ride a limitless, pleasant and sympathetic countryside ramble. Lack of fitness will not stop you from riding as far as you want to in comfort, but thrashing will.

Problems?

It must be said that mountain bike rides are not normally dangerous affairs. Generally speaking, the worst injury you will suffer is either a whopping bruise or a graze, but you should nonetheless be prepared. Rather than carry a full St John Ambulance first aid kit around with you, take a cut down version. Recommended are a small plastic bottle of TCP, or similar, and a small pad of cotton wool. These are to clean the grit and pebbles out of grazes before applying a covering plaster. Better than carrying a pack of standard-size sticky plasters which are always the wrong size and shape, take a roll of tape (paper masking tape has been used to good effect before now), and cut it to length with the small scissors or knife you thoughtfully included. Trying to tear sticky elastic bandage with your teeth whilst keeping the graze clean and not getting blood on your Rohans is tricky. A small piece of gauze or cotton wool under the tape will stop you going through the roof with shock when you eventually tear the tape off.

For big areas of skin damage, the best solution is to keep some clean clothing wrapped tight over the injury, and make for the nearest get-out as quick as possible. If you have bruised yourself, the favourite remedy is to smear the affected area with Vick or similar camphorated liniment. Really bad bruises should be splashed with water if you have any spare, then kept lightly supported by strapping. With any injuries, resist the temptation to sit down and feel sorry for yourself if you are a long way from help. Keep moving slowly to avoid stiffening up or getting cold, but without aggravating the injury if you can. The human body is a wonderfully tolerant machine, and as long as you keep warm and travel on you will have a jolly yarn to spin about your exploits.

Of course, you are not the only one who can get injured. The bike needs a first aid kit too. Rather than give a long list of what tools to take, how to wrap them and what brand to buy (this is actually covered in Chapter 5), here is a list of trail-tested bodges to keep you going.

One of the most frequent problems encountered off-road is a puncture. Rather than carry a comprehensive repair kit, on a short journey take a couple of good tubes with you. It is easier to swap a tube than mend one, especially in outdoor conditions. The punctured tube can be mended later, in more comfortable circumstances. You will then have a good tube to be taken as spare for the next ride. If the tyre is badly split, your first aid adhesive bandage stuck inside should do the trick until you get home.

The next most frequent glitch in the smooth working of any planned ride is the broken chain. The only way to deal with this is with a chain breaker. Simply remove the cracked link, and rejoin the two ends. The derailleur spring will cope with the extra tension, but remember to replace the whole chain as soon as you can. If you don't have a chain breaker you will be up the mountain without a rope, so make sure you have one in your back pocket or somewhere else safe.

The other little problem the chain breaker will help remedy is if your rear derailleur catches on a rock or branch and shears off. You will have a bike with what looks like yards of chain hanging uselessly down on the ground. Simply put the chain on the middle chainring and the middle freewheel cog; then chop and splice it to length and there you are, on your way home. If your derailleur is bent but not torn off, an adjustable spanner can be used to straighten it, but take it easy to avoid breaking anything. If the stops on the gears are not correctly adjusted, the chain will keep dropping off the edge of the freewheel and jamming into either the spokes or the frame. If this happens, try turning the wheel backwards, and the chain may dislodge itself. If not, you may need to partially remove the wheel and haul on the errant chain with both hands. Either way you'll get really dirty hands, so the moral there is to check the stops before you ride.

If your wheel develops a buckle on a ride, you can either use a spoke key to try to straighten it, or, if no spokes are broken, stand on the rim and pull it back into some semblance of trueness. Mountain bike wheels can cope with this kind of treatment, but again get it properly seen to before the next ride.

That just about covers the usual complement of problems you will come across; you may be lucky and have none for months on end, or unlucky and have all of them at one go. Luck and the way you ride will determine what happens, but if you have a chain breaker, spanner, screwdriver and 6 mm Allen key (to tighten all the cable clamps if they come loose) with you, you can travel with peace of mind as your constant companion.

Precautions

The only other useful companions, apart from that special person you met at the party last night, are the less glamorous but more practical compass and whistle. The former will help you navigate in low visibility conditions, and the latter help searchers know where you are – three short blasts then a pause is a recognised signal for help almost anywhere. You probably will not need the compass unless you are riding in strange territory, but the whistle is a handy gadget wherever you go.

And, last of all, the golden rule for all mountain bikers riding alone *anywhere* off the heavily trafficked main roads where they can be easily spotted if in trouble, is *always* tell somebody where you are going. Not doing so is foolish, can be dangerous and will definitely cause someone worry if you go missing.

If you just ride off without telling anybody your route, or a rough idea of it, you may well be gone for several hours before being reported missing. Even if you were riding at a paltry 4 mph, that would mean you could be anywhere within around 120 square miles of countryside. That is a big area for a search party to cover. If they are looking for somebody lying with a broken leg under a hedge or in a wood it could run to days. Without wishing to overstress the potential dangers, it must make sense to always tell someone where you plan to go.

On a more positive note, it must be said that many hundreds of mountain bikers head out on hundreds of rides, and come back again safely every week. Sensible preparation can turn a super ride into a fabulous one, a good ride into a famous tale, and a blurred print into a full colour glossy pin-up. If you remembered to pack the camera, that is.

7 Competitive Mountain Biking

It is said by many that competitive mountain biking goes against everything for which the activity stands. It can be seen as almost sacrilegious to hurtle through the countryside, oblivious to Mother Nature and all her doings, just to get to the finishing line before your rival. Racing against the clock has nothing to do with tranquillity, peace and beauty, it is claimed. You, of course, agree wholeheartedly, but have a nagging urge to see if you can ride up that hill quicker than your fellow. So what do you do? You brush up on the hillclimbing techniques in Chapter 3 and ride your companion into the ground.

Your companion then becomes a confirmed anti-racing mountain biker and you have to look for others to challenge. And so competitive mountain biking grows, some riders wanting to test themselves against the terrain and others wanting to prove that they are better than everybody else. This is the usual course of events: almost every mode of transport has inspired competition. From Pooh-sticks to the space race, people want to prove that their vehicle travels the fastest and the furthest.

Mountain bikers are not interested in pure speed, otherwise they would stick to motor-paced, banked velodrome races. Certainly there is a thrill to be had from shooting down a steep hillside but it is only one of the many facets of mountain biking. Neither are mountain bikers purely interested in getting dirty, though admittedly that is another part of the activity's appeal. Riding successfully through difficult terrain has its rewards, as does good navigation by map reading. Negotiating a canyon of obstacles is pleasing, but perhaps the biggest thrill of all is the feeling of being away from the roads, in an environment which suits both rider and bike. It is hardly surprising therefore, that mountain bike competitions concentrate on all these different facets. If you want to test yourself and your bike you have a whole range of events to enter.

The set-up in the UK, the US and Europe is still endearingly casual. It is not the winning that counts, it is the taking part, which includes the falling off and the head-butting of trees. But things are hotting up, sponsors are upping the odds and the prizes are becoming worth winning. Even the freebies being handed out to entrants are worth more than the entry fees. There is no doubt that mountain biking is going to evolve into a fully-fledged competitive sport.

There is, at present, no heavy book of rules and regulations to govern mountain bike competition. Whereas other cycle sports are chained by laws which have stultified their growth and development, mountain biking revels in the luxury of doing exactly what it pleases. The organisers of each different event specify their own set of rules to suit their individual aims and terrain. While some may claim that competitive mountain biking itself is contrary to the spirit of the activity, it can certainly be argued that wholesale rules and regulations go against the freedom which makes mountain biking enjoyable. The day that mountain biking gets tied down by its own laws is the day to hang up your saddle.

The most common conditions attached to mountain bike competitions relate to safety and the environment. Every organiser will require you to wear protective headgear, though they will not go into any more detail than that because, in the UK, cycle helmet safety standards have yet to filter down to grass roots level. Each organiser will decide on the day whether the headgear is safe enough for that particular event. Obviously a race down a granite cliff-face poses more threat to the well-being of your head than does a hill-climb up a heathery bank. The traditional 'leather hair-net' or 'bunch of bananas' as used by road racers is the minimum protection you should use. Hard-shell helmets with padding might be required for the toughest events.

Tyres usually have to be 1.5 in wide. The fatter the tyre, the greater the area of contact it makes with the ground and the less damage it does to that piece of ground. If mountain bikes had skinny tyres they would leave deep tracks across vegetation and wreck all but the hardest surface. Anyway, fat tyres are to your advantage because they give better grip.

Although bike maintenance is your responsibility, many competition organisers will check to make sure your bike is safe. They are not really concerned with your safety but more with the fact that if you hurt yourself it is a real bother getting you treated and explaining it to your next of kin. So they will look at the frame and fork to see if it is obviously cracked. They will try to twist loose handlebars and pull out loose wheels. They will squeeze your brakes and tug the cranks. If these items fail then you will not be allowed to take part. And why should they fail, particularly when you have followed Chapter 5 to the letter? Keep yourself in the race by keeping your bike up to scratch.

Some events, particularly long-distance races, specify that you must carry a minimum set of tools, a pump and a tyre repair kit. They may also give you some nourishment to carry. Most mountain bike races will state that you can only use one bike for the whole race. This may sound daft but, believe it or not, there are some cycle sports where you are allowed to change bikes as often as you like. Imagine being able to jump into a speedboat during the America's Cup when the wind drops, that is the equivalent of changing bikes during cyclo-cross racing. Mountain bike races test rider and machine together, on the basis that better bike-handling skills (see Chapter 3) conserve the rider's energy, the bike and its components.

Other events may specify minimum and maximum ages and all will ask you to sign a disclaimer, acknowledging that you are aware of the dangers and hold yourself responsible for your own actions. Once you have signed, you can wheel up to the start line, gaze coolly at your rivals, slip the pedals into position for maximum acceleration, squint at the distant horizon, and fall flat on your face at the first bend!

Choosing the best and most enjoyable type of event is up to you, there are many on offer.

Short Course Racing

Short course racing is great for novices, sprinters, spectators and sponsors. Short course, mountain bike races were the first to appear in the UK, in 1984, and have remained popular. They only need small areas of land and they are relatively easy to organise. They involve racing round off-road tracks up to two miles long, with up to twenty riders taking part in any one heat. Each heat can last up to twelve miles in length, or one hour plus one lap. The bigger events, such as the UK Championship Final, have many heats which lead through semi-finals to finals.

If you like short, sharp shocks then short course racing is for you. The periods of activity are sometimes only twenty minutes long, during which you must flog yourself into the ground. There are no known tactics for short course racing, you just power yourself round, avoiding the inevitable pile-ups, and hope to finish just as your energy runs out. Huge reserves of stamina are not required, merely the will to win, a small amount of explosive energy for instant response and some bike-handling skills.

The attraction of short course racing is that it is all over very quickly so you can never get left miles behind. Young riders find it is similar to BMX racing, older riders find it never goes far from the refreshment tent. Spectators get a chance to see virtually the whole of a race from one viewpoint and sponsors have the opportunity to publicise their brand to an enclosed audience.

If you want to take part in a short course race you would be well advised to practise your bike-handling skills until you can perform the manœuvres at speed. Short course races are fast and furious and the rider with the quickest reactions is often the winner. As far as your bike goes, the lighter the better because weight affects acceleration and the faster you can break from the bunch the less chance there is of getting caught in a pile-up. Short course circuits often require nothing more than ten gears, some only need five.

Short course events are very sociable because all the riders who are not taking part in a particular heat hang around the finish area and chat. You will hear tales of impossible mountain bike deeds, rumours about new components and lies about past victories. If you like mingling, taking pictures and thrashing round relatively easy terrain you can do no better than to visit a short course race.

Long Course and Wilderness Races

Long means twenty miles. Wilderness literally means wilderness. Combine the two and you have one of the toughest sporting events in the world. Imagine finding yourself on a Pennine peak, wearing nothing but skin-tight Lycra, with the mist closing in and another ten miles to ride on your mountain bike before you reach civilisation. Now imagine doing that faster than anybody else. If it still does not appeal you should stick to short course events.

The wilderness race is the traditional form of mountain bike competition. In the States, according to Hollywood westerns and cigarette advertisements, there are huge tracts of wide open space just waiting to be claimed by rough-riding pioneers. Winter ski resorts in Colorado and Vermont become mountain bike centres in the summer. Remote ranges and river valleys open up to fat-tyre freaks. The big country is perfect for the little gears of off-road cycling. In Europe, however, the population is more dense, access to land is more restricted and wilderness areas are constantly being eroded. Nevertheless, the two annual World Championships concentrate on wilderness races so they are regarded as the ultimate mountain bike events.

A wilderness race involves a mass start with all riders leaving together, following a route of at least twenty miles and returning anything up to four hours later; the time depending on mechanical difficulties and terrain. It requires stamina and good equipment. A wilderness race puts you up against the hardest terrain and under a great deal of pressure, with some events attracting hundreds of competitors. Novices should not enter wilderness races unless they have a good level of fitness derived from other cycle sports or activities.

Essentially, you have to find your own pace and try to stick to it, no matter what the ground beneath is doing. Long hills can sap your strength if you attack them too quickly. Rough rocky trails can jar your arms and back unless you plot your line carefully. Large obstacles can force you to make a mistake and drive your shins into the pedals. When you begin to tire, you may make bad judgments and pay for them with falls and spills. You may get hurt and your bike may get damaged, both of which will consume even more of your energy. So you should be as fit as you can get before taking part in a wilderness race. It is no fun lying exhausted in a dark wood, hoping that a friendly charcoal-burner will pass by with a spare derailleur in his wheelbarrow. Wilderness races pit you against the terrain and test whether you are worthy of the name of mountain biker.

It is possible to go into a wilderness race for the first time and do very well, in Europe at least. The standard of competition is always rising but it has not yet reached a level where newcomers are vastly inferior to the seasoned experts. If you have a good general level of fitness then a wilderness race is within your capabilities, as long as you have the bike-handling skills to go with it – good bike handling minimises damage to rider and bike. It is quicker to jump a ditch than to get off and wade across. It is faster to leap a log than to circumnavigate it. And, as you are racing against everyone else, you should be as quick as possible. The experts always say that the best place for gaining time is on the hills: if you can climb hills fast then you are in with a good chance in wilderness races. And if you have the nerves to let go of the brakes as you freewheel down a dried-up waterfall then nobody will be able to catch you. Wilderness races stretch you to the limit.

For a wilderness race you will need the best equipment that you can buy, equipment that will not let you down. Cheap derailleurs may be good enough for short course races but if they break half-way round a wilderness route you have got a lot of pushing to do to get home. So check out the magazine test reports, talk to other mountain bikers and find an unbiased dealer to sell you the right equipment. Of course, different terrain conditions demand different equipment: 1.5-in bald tyres will do well on flat rock courses, 2.25-in knobbly tyres will pull you through mudbaths. So check out what the course will be like, whether you will need very low gears or just a dozen across a wide range. Hub brakes would have the edge in wet conditions, short cage derailleurs would be better on really rough and rocky paths. Get as much information as possible in advance, bearing in mind that the organisers may not unveil the route of the course until the day.

You must also know your bike extremely well on a wilderness race because if anything goes wrong only you can fix it. Carrying spare inner tubes is a good idea. Some riders have two inner tubes inside a tyre when they start, one inflated and the other deflated. If the inflated tyre punctures they just pump up the second inner tube without removing the wheel. This saves them time and scares the pants off less well-prepared rivals. Get used to changing inner tubes in a hurry. Learn how to put your chain back on the rear sprockets in a few seconds. Examine the derailleurs so that re-setting them after a crunch is second nature. Carry the odd Allen key and adjustable spanner for adjustments and repairs *en route*. Anything can happen in a wilderness race but the worst only happens when you don't have the right tools to hand.

Pre-race maintenance is, of course, vital. And just as vital, though hardly ever recognised as such, is pre-race exercise. Your body gets a bit of a shock when you suddenly demand that it drives you across 25 miles of blasted heath, so you could warn it half an hour in advance with some warm-up and stretching movements. Try exercises which stretch your back, open up your thorax and warm up your legs. You will reap the rewards when you come to the first hill.

Moral support is also of great importance. If you know that there is someone waiting for you at the finish line with a warm drink and a warm heart then the inspiration to climb the final peak will be stronger. Try to get friends and family along to give you encouragement and to welcome you back from the wilderness.

Trials Events

Anyone can enter a trials meeting without fear of being left trailing the pack by five miles, because there is no pack – each rider takes part one at a time and is watched by everyone else. Trials are designed to test bike-handling skills. There is not much skill in hurtling down a hillside then grunting up the other side, that is simply brute force and ignorance. A trials meeting demands brute force, ignorance *and* skills.

A trials course is marked into short sections, some may be only three metres long, but will be recognisable because they have an obstacle in the middle. This could be a six-inch step or a two-foot diameter log. Many of the sections are set on sloping, slippery ground to make balance more difficult. Tyre traction and the right gears are important. Clever use of brakes is also a key to getting round the course without putting a foot down. Each time you put your foot down you lose a point. Trials sections are rarely approached at speed, they require deliberation and planning and are good value for spectators, in the same way as a horse-riding event. In other words, the spectators are waiting for you to fall off.

If you have learned all the tricks taught in Chapter 3, then a trials course will prove to be a lot of fun for you. If you have not, then the trials course should prove to be a lot of fun for the spectators.

If you get keen you will find that a mountain bike with a very high bottom bracket and a sloping top tube will aid your performance. In some events bikes with different sized front and back wheels will help.

Trials riding has always been a very minor part of cycle sport in general and there are a few brilliant exponents who could earn their livings as trick cyclists on the stage. Mountain bikes have added a new dimension with the new tyre technology which has been introduced and the very powerful brakes. These give excellent control in difficult situations. Trials events have a very friendly atmosphere because everyone sympathises with each other. They are a good place to learn which components are better than others. Trials events attract the real enthusiasts, but don't let that put you off.

Mountain Bike Orienteering

This activity consists of getting lost faster than anyone else and then navigating yourself home successfully. It is a direct descendant of orienteering by foot. You are given a map, a compass and a set of instructions which tell you to locate and visit several points at different corners of a wilderness area. It is up to you to plot the best route between the locations and to complete the course before everyone else. The strongest rider does not always win because he may read the map wrongly. The best navigator does not always win because he may be overtaken by a stronger rider. That leaves others with a good chance of winning and the prize is usually a pair of mudguards. All good healthy fun without the pressures of more serious racing.

Fox and Hounds

This is a favourite in the Netherlands (where mountains are few and far between) and is slowly spreading to off-road rides throughout Europe. One mountain biker sets off an hour ahead of the pack. He is the fox and the pack are the hounds. The fox marks its route with chalk and sawdust but occasionally gives the pack a choice of directions, at the junction of two bridleways for instance. If the pack makes the right choice they will come across a special mark 200 metres along the path. If they make the wrong choice there is no mark for them to find. When they have realised their mistake they must backtrack to the junction and follow the correct path. By these means the fox attempts to complete its twenty mile cross-country journey without being caught by the pack. However, astute individuals among the pack may make the correct choice of path at every junction and catch the fox before it finishes its journey. That individual is the winning hound and, as in orienteering, that hound may not necessarily be the fastest mountain biker, just the best at following a scent.

Mountain Bike Treasure Hunts

An off-road ride which involves lots of questions about local churches and not much treasure. Mind you, they are much more enjoyable than you might think and give you the opportunity to see countryside and paths which you might not otherwise find. Pub lunches and cream teas are the order of the day.

Hill Climbs and Hill Descents

Masochists flock to these small gatherings which are held on land that has been tilted to frightening angles by the inner forces of the earth. They are sometimes combined with trial events to allow the most foolhardy to display their madness. Hill climbs are performed individually and they favour riders who can pedal like crazy in impossibly low gears, while keeping their weight squarely over the front wheel and still keeping enough behind to give the back wheel traction. The aim is to ride as far as possible up steep slippery slopes. It is a great spectator event.

Hill descents are also great spectator events but have proved quite dangerous for competitors. Basically, you have to ride down a very steep hill as fast as you can. Riders attempt it one at a time and wear large amounts of protective clothing. Falls are frequent and some of them are frightening. Novices should keep well away.

Do-It-Yourself Events

Competitions can be held at the drop of a hat. Bog cycling has started in Wales; swamp surfing goes down well in Lincolnshire; log hopping takes place after every hurricane; pot-hole mountain

The sweet taste of success when you manage to complete the course.

biking has been tried; waterfall-jumping has even been attempted.

Many groups of friends organise their own contests and some go
as far as advertising them through their local cycle shop. If you
decide to arrange an event, do make sure that you have permission
from the landowner and that you are covered adequately by
insurance. First aid facilities may also be required for some events,
and for races which are held along public rights of way, including
bridleways, you will need permission from the local police.

If you win a few races you may find that clubs and teams ask you
to join them. Although team racing is not as strong in mountain
biking as it is in road racing there are some team events. But the
main advantage to be had from joining a team is that it will give
you an opportunity to train with mountain bikers of your own

standard or better. You may also find that some teams have equipment, money and expenses to offer you in return for wearing their sponsored shirt or riding their bike. Although there are no professional riders in Europe yet, there could be soon. In the US the top mountain bikers make more out of endorsing products than out of their day jobs.

Finally, although the big money and the star treatment goes to the fastest mountain bikers on the longest wilderness courses, there are other categories of riders who can win their own sections of races. Junior riders (under sixteen years of age), veterans (over 40) and women all have special prizes, and some even have their own exclusive events. Occasionally a large competition has enough prizes to give one to each and every entrant, so why not turn up, have a go and discover that pedalling yourself to your limits in the middle of some beautiful countryside can be wildly enjoyable.

8 Urban Mountain Biking

Predictions about the success and longevity of different types of transport are rarely correct. The enthusiasm to develop something faster, bigger and more expensive always gets the better of natural caution. There has been a long line of failures, from Concorde to the Sinclair C5. They may have contributed to our knowledge but they have not lived up to the claims of their original proponents. Bicycles have.

The main problem for urban cyclists is that western cities and towns have devoted themselves to motor vehicles. If the planners, economists, highways and public health authorities had more sense they would encourage everyone to sell their cars and use mountain bikes instead. The population would be fitter, the balance of payments would be improved because less cars would be imported, road maintenance costs would drop, road building costs would drop, public transport and road haulage would be more efficient, the poisonous gases would diminish and the incidence of serious traffic accidents would fall.

That is the sort of dream you have when pedalling along an upland trail, full of the joys of spring. When you get back home to your town or city, reality hits you in the bottom bracket – the world runs on four star petrol and will always do so, until not a drop is left. But look on the bright side, the more people who drive cars, the greater the freedom you have for town centre rough riding. The urban environment, no matter how unappealing it may seem, has unrivalled opportunities for the adventurous mountain biker.

Even built-up areas can present their own challenge to mountain bikes. You don't have to travel miles to blaze a new trail.

On-Road Safety

Don't get put off by traffic. Busy towns and city centres are the safest places to ride because the vehicles are travelling so slowly. You may hear of more accidents but that is because there are a lot more cyclists and children around. Slower moving vehicles mean that any injuries received in a collision are likely to be far less severe. There is more chance that you will have the vital two seconds of warning that is required to enable you to take avoiding action and minimise the consequences of the accident. The more clogged up the roads become, the better it is for you.

While screwing up your courage to leave the safety of the kerb, you should bear in mind the following advantages of a mountain bike over every other kind of bicycle. You may not have ridden on the road for several years and your last experience may have been as relaxing as a Stanley Kubrick movie – in which case a little pep talk about the superiority of a mountain bike on the road is in order.

Mountain bikes are safer than any other kind of bicycle. The rider is upright and is able to see ahead and either side quite easily. A quick glance over the shoulder will tell him what is coming up behind. Ordinary drop handlebar bikes, like racers and tourers, can induce stiff necks as riders try to look forward with their backs hunched over. On a mountain bike you ride tall, you can see over car roofs, you can stare levelly into the eyes of Transit drivers, you can assert yourself.

The location of the mountain bike rider, squarely between the front and rear axles, and the relaxed steering angle (see Chapter 2) makes for an extremely stable combination. You will find that, although the bike is neither skittish nor twitchy when steering round parked cars, the steering is positive and predictable. Pot-holes, ruts and ramps will not throw your centre of gravity into the gutter because you are well balanced. In short, a mountain bike is the cyclist's equivalent of a four-wheel drive Range Rover.

Fat tyres contribute hugely to your safety. They have a larger area in contact with the road so they are less likely to skid or slip. Fat tyres soak up the road shock before it can be transmitted to your hands and bottom and they do not puncture as frequently. They also help psychologically – whether they really do earn you more respect from drivers or whether they simply inspire more confidence in the cyclist has never been proved, but many urban mountain bikers claim that the fat tyre image gives them more space on the road and that traffic does not pass so close.

Mountain bike brakes are far superior to the ordinary caliper brakes which are fitted to other kinds of bike. Not only do they apply more stopping force to the wheels but also the good ones are more controllable; the pressure can be applied sensitively. The positioning of the brake levers and the thumbshifters on the handlebars means that your hands need only leave the bars when you are indicating. In fact, everything in the design of a mountain bike makes it the safest bicycle for on-road riding.

However, there are some drawbacks. The mountain bike is heavier than a racer or a tourer. It is slower because of the extra weight and the extra rolling resistance from the fat tyres. The handlebars on many models are wider so it is less easy to weave your way through traffic jams (which, for the record, is illegal anyway). Also, mountain bikes are brightly coloured and highly desirable so they get stolen frequently. Nevertheless, if you intend to cycle in towns and cities the mountain bike is still your safest bet.

Street Cred

There are a few simple changes you should specify when buying your urban mountain bike. If you never intend to go off-road then you are unlikely to need a machine with more than ten gears. So don't pay for the extra eight gears, the extra chainring and the overdesigned rear derailleur when ten good gears will do. Don't get super-fat tyres because they will only weigh you down and cost more money. City tyres need only be 1.5 in wide and they might have a central rib to reduce rolling resistance (at least, that is what the manufacturers claim). These central ribs also reduce the 'footprint' of the tyre so road grip is not as good. A couple of tyre manufacturers sell completely bald 1.5-in tyres specifically for urban mountain bikes. They give good grip and are noticeably faster but the soft rubber compound wears more quickly. Inner tubes should have Shraeder valves (see Chapter 2) because they can be inflated by car pumps.

Most mountain bike seat posts have a quick-release lever so that you can adjust the saddle height according to the off-road gradient you are about to tackle. The quick-release lever is not needed in the city because you will not be faced with sharp climbs and swooping descents. It is also a gift for saddle thieves (don't ask me why people steal mountain bike saddles – whole teams of psychiatrists have failed to answer that one) and it should be replaced with a traditional bolt, a Releasy cam bolt or with a HiteRite spring-loaded seat post clamp (see Chapter 9).

Quick-release wheels are also a temptation to thieves, so go for the less-expensive plain nut variety.

Get yourself a set of mudguards to avoid getting dirty stripes up the front and the back of your clothes. Make sure that the guards are long enough to cover all spray coming off the back wheel. A rear rack will be useful for panniers: cycling with a heavy weight on your back is no fun, panniers are much more efficient. And buy a good, heavy duty, U-shaped shackle lock. Shackle locks are not unbreakable but they deter the amateur thief, as long as they are locked to something solid. Some mountain bike components, however, are so desirable that no lock will prevent theft. Mountain bikers have returned to their locked machines to find that the wheels have been stolen, or even the handlebars removed. Choose sensible well-lit and conspicuous places to park your bike.

Night riding on roads requires good lights. Basically, you need a white light on the front and a red one on the back. The brighter the lights the safer you are. The easiest sort of lights are clip-on battery lights. These are tough, demountable and have a well designed retaining clamp which prevents the light from being bounced out if you venture on the bumpy stuff. You can also remove the mounting clamp easily if you want to, avoiding the 'I only left it for five minutes and now it's gone' syndrome. Even if someone does steal the mount, the back light fits neatly in your back pocket with the lens just showing. Strictly speaking this is not very legal, but it is better than nothing. The next best lights are rechargeable. These are very economical to run, but can suddenly go out when the battery is exhausted, rather than glimmering fitfully as a warning like dry batteries do. You can thus be suddenly plunged into blackness riding along the edge of a river which may lead to disastrous consequences.

The other traditional favourite of the cyclist – the dynamo – is not really suitable for mountain bikes, either in the city or elsewhere. Problems will be found in mounting it, as the tyre/frame clearances are usually greater on mountain bikes than on ordinary bikes. The tyre tread will also tend to vibrate the dynamo to pieces and give unreliable power supply due to the block pattern used. Dynamo systems are difficult to remove quickly for a spot of mud-plugging, and if you do go anywhere muddy with a dynamo attached, it will soon become a very shorted circuit.

The best place to mount your lights is clamped on the bars and, at the rear, clamped to the seat post. These positions will keep the lights and their mounting brackets from falling, or being pushed by anything, into the spokes which would ruin both lights and wheels. The other bonus is that if they do look as if they might bounce out, you can reach them without trimming your fingernails in the process.

Reflective clothing and good reflectors attached to the bike are useful in urban areas at night. The traditional across-the-chest Sam Browne reflective belt has a profound effect upon drivers because it is now associated with motorcycle police patrols. Reflective bibs keep the wind off your chest and shield your clothes from the rain. Reflectors fitted to the bicycle should be kept as clean as possible. The most useful ones are those fitted to the pedals because they attract the eyes of drivers first.

On-Road Tactics

Every country has its guidelines about behaviour on the road. These guidelines aim to encourage safe riding and minimise accidents. Unfortunately, they assume that everyone follows them. If you drive a 40-ton truck you can afford to take a few liberties with the Highway Code because you are unlikely to come off too badly in the case of a minor accident. If you drive a small car you have the acceleration to whip around other vehicles with little regard for courtesy. If you ride a mountain bike you have to take all these potential aberrations from your fellow road users into account. All the motorised vehicles have their strengths and they like to display them to 'lesser beings'. In their eyes a cyclist is a lesser being so they are tempted to edge you towards the gutter, cut you up at junctions and honk their horns when they can't get near you.

The answer is simple. You must treat urban traffic as if it is a wild dog and the way to assume mastery of a dangerous animal is to impose your will upon it. Stare it between the eyes, and it will think twice before attacking you. You must show no fear and give no quarter. As any bicycle messenger will tell you, ride aggressively and you will ride safely.

Just a small diversion here to discuss bicycle messengers. Presently they only operate in the largest cities of the world where the traffic jams are at their worst. They ride mountain bikes like there is no tomorrow, they bounce through pot-holes and are the fastest, most economical means of delivery for distances up to four miles. They even beat motor cycles.

Bicycle messengers have taken to mountain bikes for all the safety reasons mentioned at the start of this chapter, plus the fact that the frames are strong enough to withstand daily, heavy-duty batterings. They also follow a lot of unwritten laws which you would not be advised to imitate. They get paid by the amount of deliveries they make so the quicker they are, the more they earn. That is why they follow their own version of the Highway Code. Traffic lights get ignored, kerbs get jumped and one-way streets become two-way for these pedal-powered despatch riders.

You are not a despatch rider, so take it easy. The best thing to learn from the bicycle messengers is how to stake your claim to space on the road. If you dawdle along in bottom gear, wearing a brown wind-cheater and inspecting the gutter, the traffic will treat you as a piece of litter. Cars will brush past your elbow and lorries will turn across your path. Drivers only respect something which announces its strength and you have to play by their rules.

The first point in your favour is the look of your mountain bike. The fat tyres and wide handlebars give a solid impression. Your upright position makes you look bigger and more daunting than a crunched-up rider on an ordinary racer. The flashy paintwork and your luminous dungarees hit drivers right between the eyes. Look bright and ride tall in the saddle. You may not have a 2-litre, turbo-charged engine under your bonnet but you and your mountain bike spell potential.

You must use that potential. Grab the safest bit of the road and hold it, no matter what is going on behind you. In urban traffic, moving at under fifteen miles an hour, you can travel at their speed easily and keep your place in the queue. Think of yourself as a wide vehicle and take the centre of the lane, don't hug the kerb. Don't get hemmed in behind buses and lorries – move out to pass them as if you were a car. You have to be positive in all your actions and you have to be firm to keep your share of the road.

This may all sound rather daunting, but there is enormous pleasure to be had from crossing a city centre swiftly through its clogged-up arteries. You can be smug on a mountain bike in heavy traffic, and it feels great.

Inner City Riding

If you cannot get out of the industrial wasteland which lies at the heart of so many towns then do not despair. Mountain bikes are as at home on broken mortar as they are on open greensward. Once again you must make sure that you have permission from landowners before riding over a derelict site, and hard-core rubble deserves the respect shown by wearing a hardshell helmet.

Demolished buildings and old factory sites may not be the safest places in which to go hell for leather but they do offer the opportunity to practise a few of the skills you have learnt from Chapter 3.

It may not be wise to go thrashing over old spoil heaps and through half-finished excavations, but if you take things slowly and carefully you can hone your talents for trials events and for getting out of tight corners when you hit the open trail. The big drawback of riding urban wasteland is that you will get through tyres and inner tubes faster than ever before. Nails, glass, rough concrete and metal canisters are a hazard to both you and your tyres, so be prepared for punctures. Solid masonry and concrete can also make a nasty mess of your derailleur. If you are going to ride derelict land, use as much caution as you would on a cliff edge. Although help and medical aid may be closer at hand in a town centre, who is going to think of looking for you on the site of an old factory?

City mountain biking will always be a poor second to riding off the road through the country but it will complement genuine mud-plugging. So start commuting on your mountain bike, riding round to the pub on it, doing the shopping and visiting friends on it. Just think how fit you will become and how much 4-star petrol you will save.

9 Moving On – Accessories and Clothing

Why does any Mountain Biker need Accessories?

Mountain bikers need accessories to tack on to, around or inside their bikes because they want to make them *special*. They all want a bike which will not only be an instantly recognisable friend in the crush of the station bike shed, but also a bike which will fit them and their psyche like a well-worn glove.

Suppose you are a competitive soul, whether on tarmac or in the mud, you will need to set the gearing to give you maximum torque and slick changes; you will need to fit tyres that will be the ultimate in rolling assistance; and you can change the saddle to avoid chafing the inside of your furiously active thighs. All these things will change the character of the bike; it will become less like the showroom model and more like your perfect machine.

What if you are a tootler? Suppose the bike you bought, racy and gleaming, with a tucked-in riding position, is to be used for gentle meandering treks through sun-dappled woodlands, alongside chuckling reed beds and ancient village ruins? You will definitely want to slow things down a bit. Fit extra-low granny gears if they are not there already, hoick up the seating position, and fit mudguards and a rack to keep your appearance organised. Yes, accessories really are a must on any mountain bike.

Tyres

The easiest way to change the feel of any bike is to fit different tyres. What used to be, back in the old days, a choice of 'knobbly' or 'road' has now blossomed into a variety of species including 'slicks', 'high-speed road', 'dual-purpose', 'trail', 'competition' and 'expedition'. And in at least four different widths too. As you will have noted in Chapter 2, a mountain bike should have tyres of at least 1.5 in wide. Well, at a pinch you can fit anything between 1.3 in and 2.3 in, and now that ordinary bike riders are starting to fit wider, 'cross'-style tyres for touring, the distinctions have become even more blurred.

The basic rule to remember is that the thinner the tyre, the higher the pressure it will take without blowing off the rim, and the faster it will run, irrespective of tread pattern. However, thin tyres will not soak up bumps like fat tyres will, or give as much traction in tricky conditions off road. They are also more likely to slip on the rim if used at low pressure.

Tread patterns are improving by leaps and bounds as the major manufacturers realise the enormous market potential of their products. Slicks and lightly-treaded, high-speed road tyres, although they look horrendously insubstantial, run very smoothly and grip quite well both on and off road. In the dry that is. In the wet, they are still OK on tarmac but absolutely useless off-road. Their light weight and high hysteresis are ideal for high-mileage road riding with the advantage that they still soak up the pot-holes better than ordinary bike tyres.

The next category on the list towards full-blown knobblies is the centre ridge or dual-purpose tyre. These are designed to give small rolling resistance on the road by means of a solid ridge down the apex of the casing, and they have a semi-block tread either side of the ridge to give good grip off the tarmac. They are usually pretty useless at both. They still whirr and hum as the block tread rolls on the road (unless you inflate them to about 100 psi thus risking an exploding tube), and still slip as badly as slicks when off-road in the wet. Added to which the quality of centre ridge tyres is usually poor, so that even if the grip was available they are quite likely to squander it through stiff sidewalls or inferior rubber quality. They are a compromise to be avoided as soon as they wear out.

Competition and expedition tyres share similar tread patterns, based on the BMX style Compe III of old (1980). They usually have a hefty block tread on the tyre's apex, with toothed sections either side to act as self-cleaners for really mucky conditions. The tread depth is greater than any others, which makes them more grippy on loose surfaces but sets up a terrible buzzing when on tarmac. Expedition tyres only differ from competition tyres in that they have more rubber, last longer, and flick less mud up your back; they are also slightly heavier.

Lastly, trail tyres are a sort of hybrid competition-type in that they are a chunky block pattern, but designed so that the blocks overlap to stop that annoying buzzing on the road. They are really the best all-round tyre, and great for posing, too. Reasonably at home on tarmac as well as forest tracks, they do tend to clog more easily than competition treads. Cycle messengers, or despatch riders as they like to more urgently call themselves, fit trail tyres. As they earn their living from their bikes, that must be some sort of recommendation.

Pumps and Anti-flat

As a serious mountain biker you need a pump. Not only for those occasions when your tyre has an argument with a thorn and loses, but also for when you are attacked by rabid dogs. As is usual with most bikes, you will find your new bike is not automatically supplied with this most essential piece of equipment.

Any of the high pressure two-stage types are good. These usually have a camlock fixing which squeezes itself on to the valve, rather than the little rubber hose as found on regular pumps. Make sure the pumps you choose fits the valve type on the bike. It can be either Woods, Presta or Schraeder (see Chapter 2). Also check the pump mounting. It is no good having a frame-fit pump which drops off every time you put the bike on your shoulder, or one which requires a pump peg or two when there are none on your frame. Hardened mountain bikers either use BMX pumps which strap to the frame, or they use insulating tape to stick pumps to a handy length of frame tubing, which is not a very pretty alternative.

If you really cannot be bothered with pumping, you could invest in some of the liquid anti-flat preparations which are available. The idea behind these is that when a hole is made in the tube, the air rushes to it and squirts out. So if you put something sticky inside the tube, the air will rush the cloggy stuff into the hole and with any luck it will stay there and seal the puncture. The compounds used are generally some sort of anaerobic sealing liquid with a fibre compound in suspension. Two disadvantages are apparent with these fluids. Firstly, they can be difficult to get into the tube without clogging the valve, and secondly, if they do seal a puncture, they can seal the tube to the tyre as well. Apart from those little snags, anti-flat sealants are generally a good idea, even if they do add to the overall weight somewhat.

Saddles

Two schools of thought apply to the role of the saddle on a mountain bike. One maintains that as you spend so little time sitting down, being a vigorous thrusting sort of rider, the saddle does not really matter much. This school buys cheap saddles made of plastic, and wrecks them regularly by falling off, landing heavily from jumps and so on. Such people are philistines and obviously never ride more than ten miles at one go. The second school, the caring thoughtful type, go for a good quality leather or leather-covered nylon saddle. These saddles are stronger, more comfortable and more expensive, but they always last longer. Most mountain bikes, manufactured with an eye on the balance sheet, come with the first type of saddle.

When choosing a replacement saddle, look for strong mounting rails, both where they fit into the saddle base and where they bend. A broken saddle rail can be very dangerous if you land heavily. Some solid leather saddles have springs; these are obviously more comfortable but weigh a lot more and are generally wider at the back. This can cause rubbing on your thighs if you do a lot of high-speed pedal work. They are thus more suitable for expedition riding, when comfort, not weight, is at a premium, than racing. Some saddles are designed specifically for the female pelvic structure. Whichever type of saddle you choose, a saddle cover is a good idea. This keeps the wet off the leather surface which will become stiff if left damp and muddy for long periods, as does the rider's bottom.

Also in the seating department, one very useful accessory is the HiteRite. This is a gadget designed to allow you to change your saddle-height without getting off the bike, even when you are riding. One end clamps to the seat post, the other to the top of the seat tube and the two are connected by a strong spring which pushes the saddle up against the riders weight when the Q/R lever is loosened. This sounds somewhat implausible and in practice happens rarely. The HiteRite does stop light-fingered folk from stealing your saddle when parked up outside the local bistro though, so on that score alone it is a highly recommended item.

Bars and Grips

Two things you will probably want to alter sooner or later on your mountain bike are the bars and grips. The first mountain bikes used to come with what were called 'bullmoose' bars; which were one piece, triangulated and very wide. They were great for plunging down steep Californian fire trails, but required the rider to develop arms the length and width of an orang-utan. Bullmoose bars have now been superseded by two-piece bars that give a much better choice of riding position. Most two-piece bars are narrower, making them better for traffic-jamming, but they still tend to be a little low for some touring applications. If you prefer a more sit-up-and-beg posture, fit a swan-neck stem with as much rise as you can, and bars with about 2 in of rise in them. This gives you a higher, less neck-cricking hand-grip position, but they can be swung forward and down if you need to go for it at any time.

Grips are still going through the experimental and innovatory process. They range from the particularly uncomfortable yet hygienic mushroom grips which are made up of lots of thin plate-like rings wrapped around the end of the bar, to super sorbo rubber grips. These are initially comfortable, but as they soak up your sweat become totally microbe infested, stink, rot and fall to pieces. About the best are the medium hard, rubber grips. These cushion the wheel shocks to a large extent, yet stay useful and comfortable for quite a long time. Incidentally, if you are trying to remove stubborn grips, push a very thin screwdriver down the open end, then pour water in and twist them. They will come off very easily.

Lighting

The easiest sort of lights are battery lights. The cheapest to run are rechargeables. Dynamo lights are not suitable. You will have to choose carefully how robust and illuminating you require your lights to be – read the lighting section in Chapter 8.

Mudguards

If your bike is to be used as your main form of transport, then it is no good saying to yourself that as a macho mountain biker you don't

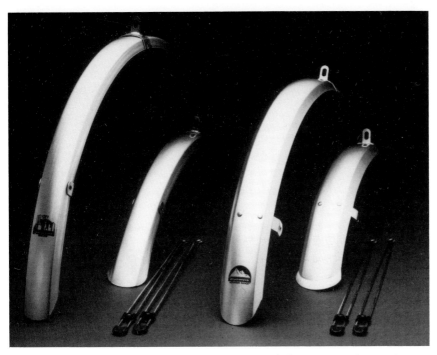

Mudguards need to be wide to cover fat tyres and the stays are heavy duty to cope with sticks and rocks.

need to fit mudguards. Apart from the obvious mucky consequences, strictly speaking, Mr Plod could tear you off a strip as well. It is a legal requirement to fit mudguards, but in practice the boys in blue are too busy arresting traffic to bother with the mud in your eye.

However, mudguards are very useful accessories. The most widely fitted are the laminated type: a thin, plastic/metal/plastic composite. The good thing about these is that they can bend and twist without shattering, but they can jam the wheel up if a branch gets caught in the spokes. Any mudguard needs to be at least 2 in wide to be of any use, and have at least $\frac{3}{4}$ in clearance between it and the tyre to avoid excess mud clogging. If possible, two stays should be provided on each side plus a top centre fixing. Less than this and the whole lot starts to rattle around quite easily. Mudguard length is quite important too. You will still get the stripey back syndrome if the back one is too short, so make sure it covers as much as possible. Too short at the front ensures that your shoes, boots or plimsoles get all the front wheel run-off channelled into them. Unpleasant.

Some so-called 'city' guards look really racy, but are so short that they are not really worth the effort of fixing them on. Mudflaps front and rear can be quite useful if you can get hold of them. If you cannot, then flaps made of old tractor inner tubes or similar are very street cred.

Racks

If you want to carry more than a tube of Smarties and a spare pair of socks when you are out and about, you will do well to look at a rack for your bike. The extra carrying capacity a rack will give you can be quite surprising. You can put panniers on it, carry a dog in a box, take friends to parties, or transport the whole week's shopping back from the supermarket. But you will need a rack to match the bike. If the seat stays have twin mounting points on them, make sure the rack you choose will fit, before you leave the shop.

Popular choice, at present, favours the aluminium alloy rack for lightness and strength. The alternative – steel – is generally heavier but stiffer and less prone to catastrophic failure. The other trendy choice is a low-rider rack. This holds the bags lower down than the usual position, which the manufacturers claim results in a more stable ride when heavily loaded.

The choice is yours, but whichever you go for, make sure that the rack will cope with the bags and fixings you intend to use, as some types are incompatible. One other point to watch out for on bikes fitted with cantilever brakes is that the rack and the luggage it will carry do not interfere with the brake calipers. Inefficient braking or holes in the bags can result if there is any rubbing. When mounting racks, always use a separate set of mounting holes if there are any, or put them on the inside of mudguard stays if there is only one set of holes. Racks bolted on the outside of a set of mudguard stays always come loose.

Luggage

Nothing makes a mountain bike look more purposeful than a full set of expedition luggage. An ordinary road bike looks totally swamped, skinny and overwhelmed, by huge panniers and a full complement of water bottles, camping gear and spares. A mountain bike looks ready for business wearing the same gear. So go for the chunkiest you can find. Strapping extra bits and bobs on the outside with bungees is not as secure as carrying them safely in the bags. It also looks uncool.

Avoid the limp, lightweight, nylon cheapies, they are not tough enough for life on the trail. The bags you use will need to be capable of being skidded on, rubbed against gateposts and dunked in the occasional stream, all the while keeping your goods dry. Some of the best are made from Cordura, a sort of modern equivalent of good old cotton duck as used in Thirties' hostelling bags. Not only is Cordura waterproof, but it will keep its shape and is therefore less likely to become snagged on protruding bits of the countryside.

Panniers are available which convert to rucksacks when you want to leave the bike. These are expensive but a good idea if you plan to combine cycling and walking on your expeditions.

There are other specialist bags that you can get for short rides. Small purpose-built rucksacks, handlebar bags, and bags which strap under the saddle. The latter are neat, light, look good in the showroom and get plastered in filth as soon as you ride the range. Handlebar bags are useful for carrying a map and light items, but

When riding through scrub or low branches a backpack does not catch in the vegetation like panniers.

too much weight at this level makes the steering very pendulous. Rucksacks are good if you are going to be doing a lot of bike lifting, or just want to use the bike to transport you plus gear to a destination, such as the foot of a local climb. They do make you very sweaty though, often rub your shoulders, and can limit you and the bike's joint manœuvrability. Don't carry too much in them.

Security

Locking the bike up and how to avoid getting it stolen are dealt with in passing in Chapter 8, but there are a few little accessories which will help you avoid being bikeless.

The Releasy replaces the quick release lever you usually flip with your finger – to loosen either the wheel or the saddle – with a socket head screw. The socket head screw can then be operated easily with an Allen key which you carry in your pocket. A casual thief is unlikely to have an Allen key about their person.

The opportunist component thief may be deterred if you make the removal of accessories a difficult and lengthy process, but the determined 'steal-to-order' bicycle thief is a different story. He will be professional, working with a team and determined to take your bike. The only way to keep out of the insurance statistics is to buy a very strong and visible lock. If the bike is going to take more than five minutes to remove, and is in full view of passing public, then the professionals are less likely to bother with it. The best locks for deterrent value are shackle U-locks. They look very tough, usually are, and are easy for you to operate. They often come with a mounting clip for the frame for when they are not in use, but they are heavy and can make total security (locking front and back wheel as well as frame to a solid object) difficult to achieve because of their limited size. The next best are toughened chain locks with a whopper of a padlock. These can be wrapped round, through and across every bit of the bike, but are harder to carry. They also stretch around lampposts more easily and, as railings in dimly lit areas are frequently sawn through to steal a bike, lampposts must be a better bet.

The other thing, not really an accessory, which you can buy to help prevent your bike being stoken is a can of black spray paint. If you can bring yourself to do it, covering the glossy paintwork with streaks of matt black will make the thoroughbred which lurks beneath look like an old tank. Nobody wants to nick a bike with streaky black rims, brakes and splodges all over the frame. The messier the job the better.

Gizmos

Before you finally leave the shop and whilst you still have some plastic credit left, a quick flip through various other useful gizmos.

Chainstay protectors stick on the frame where the chain would otherwise rub all the paint off when rough riding. Some have extra little tangs to stop the chain from getting jammed down between the chainring or tyre and the chainstay. These are useful and cheap, but make sure the frame is squeaky clean before you stick them on. Otherwise they drop off immediately.

Quick-release chain links can be fitted to make chain removal easier, but may tend to weaken the drive chain. Select carefully here, and check their condition regularly.

Foam padding for the crossbar helps to stop severe crotch-bruising in a crunch situation. It can enhance the appearance of the bike and it also helps when carrying the bike on the shoulder.

One-key release bolts for the cranks let you pull the cranks off

Removable links speed up chain removal but do not do away with the need for a chainbreaking tool completely.

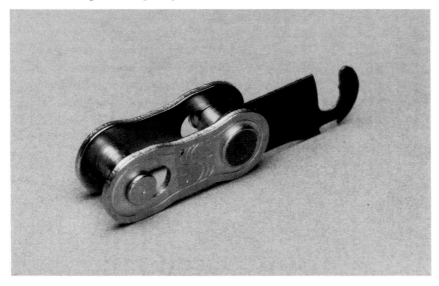

the bottom bracket spindle (or tighten it up) using only a 6 mm Allen key. They are a must on any bike, being quick, easy to fit and saving you the weight (about $\frac{1}{2}$ lb) of an extractor tool in the toolkit.

A speedo/milometer is great fun, keeps you interested in what is going on distance-wise and is not over expensive. Make sure you get an easy to fit, waterproof model.

Walkman/compact disc players, which are absolutely forbidden by all serious cycling groups for riders in town or heavy traffic, are worn everywhere by thousands of mountain bikers. They can stop you hearing what is going on, but they also help drown the cacophony of internal combustion all around. They can be positively spiritual with the right music in the right place up in the hills and, used selectively, are highly recommended. Another Japanese accessory – a camera – can help recall those high and low spots in your mountain biking career. Compact autofocus models are most impressive, but throw-away ultra lightweights that come with a pack of three films do the job just as well in most instances. You won't worry if you sit on them either.

The best place to buy your gadgets is the bike shop where you bought the bike. They will know what will fit and what will not. If you buy them at the same time as the bike, expect to get some of them free, and fitted too if you are lucky. Second-hand bargains are to be had, but bearing in mind what most mountain bikers do to the stuff they ride, *caveat emptor*. The other way to buy accessories is through a mail order house. The problem with these is that they do not always have in stock just what you want. If they don't, it can take weeks of phone calls, letters and waiting until your new seat bolt arrives. It may be quicker to travel to the nearest major town to a specialist shop.

Clothing

If you have read through Chapter 6 you will know that the best clothing strategy is to layer. Wear light cotton or synthetic long-limb garments next to the skin. These will help to soak up sweat and keep a layer of warm air next to your body. The number of layers you need will obviously depend on the weather, your planned route and for how long you are going. The important thing to remember is that you must keep your trunk, or torso, warm. If your core temperature drops, hypothermia can set in and you could be

Unofficial regulation clothing includes extremely untrendy jeans, checked shirt, cap worn backwards and tough boots.

in grave danger. Use T-shirts, sweatshirts, jumpers and so on, topped with a windproof layer if it is cold out. If it is a roasting summer day all you need is something to stop you getting sunburnt, say a skinsuit or similar. But remember that a sweaty body on top of a windy hill, even when the sun is very hot, will chill quickly. Wear something to keep the core warm even on hot days.

One choice you are faced with when buying your mountain bike attire is simple. You can choose to be a popinjay or a camouflagee. The former will go for skin-tight, pink racing tights worn under dayglo bib shorts, tastefully matched with multicoloured, woolly socks and climbing boots and an outrageously cool pair of shades to round off the effect. Other people will either see you and run, or ask you where you got the gear, man.

Camouflagees go for the russets, pastels and Earth Mother styling. That is not to say they are shapeless, just that another pack of wholewheat energy bars stuffed in one of many voluminous pockets would not spoil the cut of their jib. However, veterans of the local ramblers' club might still say hello despite you being on a bike.

Both approaches have their plus points. As a popinjay going out for a blast with some mates, you don't want to be encumbered by heavy clothing. Your energy conversion rate will keep you warm, and you will be travelling light and fast – no pockets are required. If it rains, then you will get soaked, but being thinly clad will soon dry off when you find shelter. You can be light, lean, self-sufficient and luminous.

As a camouflagee on the ramble trail, you may stop, start, dream awhile, need a snack or a thousand and one other things which take your self-indulgent fancy. You will not be constantly keeping yourself warm with rapid exercise, so dressing more thickly is very sensible. Your top layer needs to be wind- and waterproof, preferably permeable like Goretex so that you don't boil inside when you go up a hill. Your clothes will need to conserve your heat when you are stationary and so need to cover you all over. You will probably be carrying camera, notebook and bird-spotting guide, so pockets are a must. And you don't want to be too bright; keep the beta waves slow and low.

Tops

Skin tops are fairly warm, but make sure they are long enough to cover your kidneys at the back. Don't wear thick woollies. They are heavy to start with and even more so when wet. Goretex tops are good but incredibly expensive, whereas a cheapish thin cotton, zip-up jacket will keep the wind out and dry quickly if wet. Or you could proof it with wax spray, or similar, if you want to be a yuppie. Heavy thermal jackets are to be avoided unless they have ventilating flaps somewhere, usually under the armpits. Leather jackets are great for crashing in as they really protect you well, but they are hot and seldom long enough to protect the lower back.

Bottoms

Leg coverings are almost essential for mountain biking. Even when racing, thin tights will give that little extra protection against abrasions. Other race favourites are skinshorts worn over the tights, to make even more colourways than before. General tootling calls for more supportive wear. Whatever you go for, make sure it is either waterproof or will dry quickly. Thick denim simply gets heavy and cold when wet and stays damp for ages. Trousers with ties or straps at the bottom will be baggy enough to give you

Long cycle shorts with chamois leather crutch inserts stop chafing and soreness. Ordinary shorts with thick seams are uncomfortable, particularly when riding rough tracks. Some riders wear shorts under ordinary trousers.

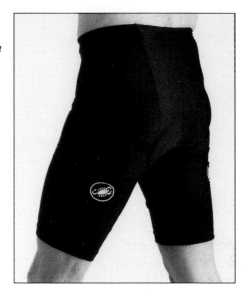

freedom of movement but will keep themselves out of the chain when you are pedalling. Army surplus shops have dozens of styles.

Socks

Socks are a potential ride-ruiner. Get the wrong sort and your feet will be sore, the wrong temperature and probably bruised. Go for thick acrylic, wool and cotton mixes. They keep your feet warm, protect your ankles from knocks and absorb sweat. Make sure that they are long enough to come about half-way up your calves. You can then tuck your trousers into the tops, giving an extra layer of protection. Avoid nylon socks at all costs. They rub, make you sweat and give no support at all. Leg warmers and Goretex socks can help make poor sock choice bearable, so check them out too.

Footwear

Strong footwear is the order of the day on a mountain bike, to cope with the pedal surfaces if nothing else. Some support should be given to the ankle and shin. Lightweight walking boots seem best suited to tootling but can cramp the ankles. Cut-down baseball boots are best for racing, unless you are very well-heeled in which case go for custom-built mountain bike boots. Also available at the local army surplus shops, high-top trainers are great, being both light yet supportive. Made with cotton panels, they don't last long

Opposite *Casual clothes are practical and less expensive than specialist off-road garments.*

but are light and dry quickly if dunked. Some specialist Goretex boots are available which are, as usual, very good but very pricey.

Extras

To be smart, and to be able to see properly, you will also need goggles. Mountaineers' specs look most impressive, industrial safety goggles are pretty good, but tinted, wrap-around shades are for the popinjays. Goggles keep bugs out of your eyes and stop them watering.

Hats are discretionary when mountain biking. Peaked models, as supplied by American agricultural companies, are cool, knitted acrylic as worn by ordinary cyclists are uncool. Leather flying helmets have some adherents. For helmet advice check out Chapter 7.

Gloves are a good idea. They keep your hands either warmer, or less sweaty than otherwise, and keep your knuckles from being whipped by passing twigs. Fingerless mittens are not really recommended, as you still get knuckle-whip and cold digits. Silk motorbike undermitts can be very good in cold weather.

It is your Choice

The wonderful thing about mountain bikes is that you don't have to have the very latest gadget or bolt-on to make your bike stand out from the crowd. In the very best *Blue Peter* tradition, you can fashion a mud scraping, oil retentive, water repellent, chain-saving spoke protector from a washing-up liquid bottle if you want to, and still have the best one for miles around.

10 *A Great Adventure*

Do you have a nagging urge to do something bigger, to ride up something higher and to achieve something more impressive?

How about a real mountain or two? After all, the bikes are called *mountain* bikes and, unless they contravene the Trade Descriptions Act, they should jolly well take you up a mountain.

If you have dreams of achieving glory and fame by riding your bike to the top of a renowned peak you can forget it. The big summits have been conquered already and even the first to the tops did not hit the headlines. The problem is that bicycle expeditions are regarded as worthy but eccentric. If somebody runs up Everest without oxygen they are fêted, and rightly so. But when two cousins, such as Nick and Dick Crane, mountain bike up Kilimanjaro, their feat is barely heralded. They get a mention in the *Guinness Book of Records* and the world moves on. It is as if the mountain bikes had given them some unfair advantage. While expeditions such as the one which crossed Iceland using two canoes, an inflatable raft, two micro-lights, two motorised ski-bobs, a Land Rover and a light aircraft got the attention of documentary-makers, mountain biking over the Andes is ignored. The only way to achieve fame from mountain biking would be to have a high-tech support team and a mobile canteen to feed a film crew along with you.

Opposite *Dick and Nick Crane wearing clothes for hostile conditions on their ride up Kilimanjaro.*

The first thing to learn is that a mountain bike expedition will not gain credence among non-mountain bikers. Invariably they will ask why you are taking a mountain bike at all, why don't you just walk up? They seem to think that riding a mountain bike would make the journey less pleasant. But you know better and this is when you realise that really you are not doing it for public acclaim, you are doing it because you enjoy mountain biking.

The next step is to decide what would be the most enjoyable and satisfying challenge. Choose a target which is realistic and probably achievable, not because failure to succeed is a bad thing but because an unreachable goal could force you into danger. The closer you get to your chosen summit the harder it becomes to turn back. You may be tempted to take risks which would otherwise seem obviously too dangerous. Mountain biking down the inside of Mount Etna would certainly be something to shout about, but only if you came out alive!

At the last count there were twenty-three expeditions cycling their various ways over and among the Himalayas. Records are being claimed, heroic tales are being rehearsed and the roof of the world is ringing to the sound of missed gear changes. Shangri-La has been mobilised by fat tyres and even mysterious Kathmandu has a mountain bike shop – no spares, just the bikes.

Our own story illustrates the point that you don't have to join a flashy expedition nor find a publicity-conscious sponsor to make a cycle tour of somewhere like the Great Himalaya. You don't even have to be very fit – we weren't. All you need is a minimum of two weeks and around £650. A support team of porters, cooks and doctors is always useful, but if you use your common sense you will get on better without them. This is how we made the trip with next to no preparation and no clear idea of where we were going.

We cleaned up a two-year-old Muddy Fox Pathfinder and built a weird bike called the Rattus K2 out of the astoundingly unsuccessful Reynolds 531 SL aerodynamic tubing. Any mountain bike with enough low gears can make the trip. We took a ten-year-old Blacks Good Companion tent, minus fly sheet, and two sleeping mats and Nomad Navajo sleeping bags. Clothing was based around Thermalite underwear, Castelli shorts and baseball caps to keep the sun off.

Thai International airlines bagged our bikes for free and deposited us in Delhi at midnight. A word of advice here: do not take a taxi

from Delhi airport at midnight. We did and it cost a fortune as well
as dropping us at an expensive, 'Western' hotel, costing £15 a night,
bootprints on the sheets gratis. It is better to stay within the womb
of the new airport terminal, sleeping if you can, and re-assemble
your bike at dawn for a cool ride into town where a complete stranger
will most probably accost you and try to sell you a ticket to Kashmir
for £11, on a coach leaving that evening and taking twenty-four
hours. Load your bike on to the coach roof along with your baggage,
take water bottles on to the coach for refreshment and try to ignore
the Hindi video which is repeated three times during the night. Ear
plugs are recommended.

Twenty-nine hours later, five more than advertised, at around
midnight you will arrive in Srinagar, the capital of Kashmir. If it
is low season the houseboat owners will literally fight each other to
gain your custom. Fix a deal quickly but never pay more than £5 a
night for a twin room on a Class A houseboat, including breakfast
and supper, private bathroom, dining room, saloon, sun deck and
your own personal minder. A good minder will protect you from
the hassle and haggle that keep Kashmir alive. He will also try to
sell you boat trips, papier mâché and hashish on behalf of his
extended family and of the houseboat's owner.

We spent two days recovering from our coach journey, revelling
in the luxury and wondering at the serenity of the lake on which
we stayed, with its colonial houseboats, hundreds of taxi boats and
dozens of floating merchants. Beyond the lakes are the snowy
mountains and, with bikes checked over, we set off, cycling from
Srinagar to Leh, the capital of Ladakh in the northernmost part of
India. The route is 270 miles long, crosses the Great Himalaya at
11,575 ft and then rises to two more passes at 12,022 ft and 13,749 ft.

Everyone in Kashmir said it would be impossible. They said the
Himalayan pass was blocked with snow for six more weeks. We
guessed that they wanted us to stay in Kashmir longer and we
reckoned the only way to discover the truth would be to go up and
take a look. On the first day we cycled for eight hours, leaving the
plain beneath us and following a surfaced road up the green and
pleasant Sind valley for maybe fifty miles. For food we cooked
vegetables and bought hard-boiled eggs, biscuits, cheese and bread.
Our daily bill was around £1 each. The fear of illness drove us to
iodise every drop of water that we drank for the entire trip, though
we still succumbed to Delhi belly. Neither fasting nor drugs cured

the problem so we just learned to live with it. Luckily we had taken with us five rolls of toilet paper.

The bicycles excited a lot of attention. Within ninety seconds of stopping anywhere in Kashmir, even in seemingly deserted areas, between twenty and fifty people (nearly all male) would surround us and stare, even though we were doing nothing whatsoever. Once interest in the gears and tyres had subsided we often found ourselves the butt of their jokes. We had nothing to sell or to show them so we must be there for their amusement, they reasoned. With bad grace we would cycle off and our initial enthusiasm for greeting everyone with a cheery *Salaam!* soon faded into sullen silence.

On that first night away from Kashmir we camped, providing entertainment for an entire village and all its stray dogs. On the second day we learned that it was wisest to ride from 6 am to 2 pm in order to avoid heat exhaustion in the afternoon sun. That night an officer at a tiny army post on the edge of the snow-line invited us to stay in a vacant dug-out in return for allowing him to ride our bikes till dusk.

When you reach the snow line, as we did early on day three, it makes sense to cover up your entire body, smear your face with zinc or glacier cream and avoid the sun and the snow glare as much as possible. We left little gaps by accident. (Jeremy's wrists are now scarred where the shirt sleeves failed to meet the gloves.) Our ears turned to crispy bacon and our noses shone like dying volcanoes. All that in four hours. Sunglasses are essential.

The route had been cleared to 11,000 ft where we overtook the snowplough and camped in solitude, apart from a train of thirty-five porters who trekked across the snow and down to the woods at the bottom of the valley. When we heard the avalanches that night we realised why they camped in the woods. It was the safest place to be. If you reach Baltal in spring don't camp by the road, the fear of being smothered by 20,000 tons of snow will stop you from sleeping.

The next day we were tired and nervous. We rose late and the snow was soft, making cycling impossible. We still had seven miles of snow to cross before we would reach the top of the first pass and we had no idea how much snow lay beyond that into Ladakh. We did what you should do in those circumstances: we weighed the risks against our skills and resources. Then we turned around and freewheeled back into Kashmir.

That is probably the difference between expeditions and trips. On an expedition there is an aim, a method and a rational answer to the question 'Why?'. On such a trip as ours, and yours probably, the aim was to have a jolly good time and to stop if we were no longer enjoying ourselves. So turning around was no great disappointment; we had gone as far as we dared and decided not to dice with death just to get our names in the 'missing' column of *The Times of India*. Besides, we knew we had a couple of weeks to play with and if the snow receded we could have another go.

Free of the burden of a challenge, we sped around the lakes and mountains of Kashmir, getting fit and feeling easy; experiencing the real beauty of cycling, which enables you to choose when to stop and what to look at. You are in control.

Until you stop to buy radishes in Magam, that is. This was the point at which the pressures of being a curiosity became unbearable. When a big enough crowd had gathered the shopkeeper decided to play games at our expense and he proved to be the last straw. We fled to Srinagar and hid on the houseboat for a week. Whether you choose to do the same depends on your tolerance of attention-seeking and provocative Kashmiris.

We spent time servicing the mountain bikes on the end of a private pontoon in the middle of a lake. So far the trip had not affected the frames or the components to any noticeable degree. The Sturmey Archer hub brakes on the Rattus K2 were bedding in nicely and a new pair of sealed jockey wheels were fitted to the rear derailleur to be tested for the manufacturer. The Shimano components were unmarked and only needed lubrication which was just as well because we had a very basic toolkit in order to keep the weight down, the heaviest items being spare tyres. If the tyres had shredded themselves on rocky descents, as we had been warned, the bikes would have been useless without spares. And 26 × 2.25-in Panaracer Knobblies were hard to come by in Kashmir.

A week doing nothing is sufficient rest so then you can stash your bike on a bus and return to Baltal to find that the snow has retreated, as we did. The route had turned to mud and rock and the wind was high. The only danger was the cold and our lack of energy, so we camped 200 metres short of the pass, called the Zoji La, and ate a hearty meal with two New Zealanders who were walking to Ladakh. Out of the darkness came five soldiers with a briefcase who told us that there were eight miles of snow ahead.

You can cycle over the snow, when it is frozen hard, early in the morning and at night. Just follow the footprints of the trekkers and gape at the peaceful mountains – not too long or your palate will burn from snow glare. At 9 am the snow will soften and you will have to push and shove your bike the last couple of miles. By midday you will reach the other side and you can swoop down the hairpins into the giant gravel quarry that is Ladakh's high altitude desert. The Great Himalaya is behind you.

You should cycle into Ladakh while the Zoji La is blocked with snow; as soon as the road is opened convoys of hundreds of vehicles take the military and the tourists from Srinagar to Leh. When the pass is blocked you will have the great, glorious bone-dry valley to yourself.

We shot through Ladakh, travelling fast. The ten-mile uphill climbs to the next two passes took three hours each, with a touch of altitude sickness which disappeared after a half-hour rest. The ten-mile descents on the other side of the passes were thrilling – 40 mph or more, freewheeling and zigzagging round the hairpins. The scenery was unearthly and the Ladakh people – people who have nothing but a few goats, a tiny field of barley and the odd apricot tree – are the kindest and most dignified you will ever meet.

For the equivalent of 40 pence we stayed in a cave-like mud-hut hotel opposite a huge rock carved into a likeness of Buddha a thousand years earlier. For the equivalent of 50 pence plus a ride on our bikes the monks let us stay at Lammayuru monastery. The village bank at Saspul put us up for the night and fed us for nothing. People will be interested mainly in the condition of the snow at the Zoji La pass, they will quietly consider your bicycle and they will wish you 'good day' with a smile. Not for them the oafish manners of Kashmir.

The exhilaration of freewheeling and our general tiredness led to a few minor errors. Half-way along a seven-mile straight across the desert into Nimmru we heard a noise like a screaming jet plane. It was a badly-packed pannier rubbing against a rear tyre. When eventually we reached a very short piece of uphill it was difficult to get into the right gear quickly. In the haste to change down the chain was wrenched and one link gave up the ghost. Fortunately, our toolkit contained a link extractor and a short length of spare chain.

On our final day we hit a bad patch, a six-mile climb of which we could see every mile before us with no hairpins to keep us guessing. Just short of the top we met a group of roadmenders, men and women, having lunch. They invited us to taste their yak-butter tea and barley flour. They may not be there when you pass through, but somewhere along the road from Srinagar to Leh, across the Great Himalaya, you will come quite close to euphoria. We did.

The Mountain Biking Directory

Useful Addresses

This body of information was correct at the time of publishing. The names
and addresses which it includes may be of use to novice and experienced
mountain bikers alike, as sources of further information and participation.
Telephone numbers are included for organisations where they are readily
available.

Mountain Bike and Bicycle Organisations in the UK

Mountain Bike Club
3 The Shrubbery
Albert Street
St Georges
Telford
Shropshire
TF2 9AS
Tel: 0952 610158

British Cyclo-Cross Association
8 Wakeley Close
Biggin Hill
Kent

Cross-Country Cycling Club
5 Station Road
Ford
Arundel
West Sussex

Cycle Campaign Network
Tress House
Stamford Street
London
SE1
Tel: 01–928 7220

Cyclists' Touring Club
69 Meadrow
Godalming
Surrey
GU7 3HS
Tel: 04868 7217

Friends of the Earth
26–28 Underwood Street
London
N1 7JQ
Tel: 01–490 1555

Rough-Stuff Fellowship
9 Liverpool Avenue
Southport
Merseyside
PR8 3NE

Scottish Mountain Bike Club
26 Howe Street
Edinburgh
EH3 6TG

International Mountain Bike Organisations

National Off-Road Bicycle Association (U.S.A.)
PO Box 1901
Chandler
AZ 85244

National Off-Road Bicycle Association (Canada)
2205 Ontario St
Vancouver
BC

Association of French Mountain Bikers
Patrick Hennet
31 Avenue Berthet
95110 Sannois
France

Country Activities Organisations in the British Isles

Association of Lightweight Campers
c/o 11 Grosvenor Place
London
SW1W 0EY

British Horse Society
British Equestrian Centre
Stoneleigh
Kenilworth
Warks
CV8 2LR
Tel: 0203 52341

British Mountaineering Council
Crawford House
Precinct Centre
Booth Street East
Manchester
M13 9RZ
Tel: 061-273 5835

Byways & Bridleways Trust
9 Queen Anne's Gate
London
SW1H 9AS

Council for National Parks
45 Shelton Street
London
WC2H 9HJ
Tel: 01–240 3603

Countryside Commission
John Dower House
Crescent Place
Cheltenham
Glos
GL50 3RA
Tel: 0242 521381

Countryside Commission for Scotland
Battleby
Redgorton
Perth
PH1 3EW
Tel: 0738 27921

Forestry Commission
231 Corstorphine Road
Edinburgh
EH12 7AT
Tel: 031-334 0303

Long Distance Walkers' Association
29 Appledown Road
Alresford
Hants
SO24 9ND
Tel: 0421 29 3226

National Trust
36 Queen Anne's Gate
London
SW1H 9AS
Tel: 01-222 9251

National Trust for Scotland
5 Charlotte Square
Edinburgh
EH2 4DU
Tel: 031-226 5922

Open Spaces Society
(Commons, Open Spaces and
Footpaths Preservation Society)
25a Bell Street
Henley-on-Thames
Oxon
RG9 2BA
Tel: 0491 573535

Ordnance Survey
Romsey Road
Maybush
Southampton
Hants
SO9 4DH
Tel: 0703 634271

Ramblers' Association
1/5 Wandsworth Road
London
SW8 2JL
Tel: 01–582 6826

Scottish Youth Hostels Association
7 Glebe Crescent
Stirling
FK8 2JA
Tel: 0786 2821

Trail Riders Fellowship
29 Anderson Drive
Kettering
Northants
NN15 5DG
Tel: 0604 486665

Woodland Trust
Westgate
Grantham
Lincs
NG31 6LL
Tel: 0476 74297

Youth Hostels Association
Trevelyan House
8 St Stephens Hill
St Albans
Herts AL1 2DY
Tel: 0727 55215

**Youth Hostels Association
Ireland (An Oige)**
39 Mountjoy Square
Dublin 1
Tel: Dublin 01–745734

**Youth Hostels Association
Northern Ireland**
56 Bradbury Place
Belfast
Tel: 0232 24733

Mountain Bike Companies

We have listed as many addresses as possible of the UK companies which have branded mountain bikes for sale. We have not attempted to list the different models from each company, nor have we distinguished between multi-national companies and small framebuilders. If you have an enquiry about a specific brand of mountain bike write to the relevant address below.

Ammaco
Unit 1F
Deacon Industrial Estate
Forstal Road
Aylesford
Maidstone
Kent

Tom Avon
7 Chessels Street
Bedminster
Bristol
Avon

Barretto's
7 Dean Hill
The Broadway
Plymstock
Plymouth
Devon

British Eagle
Eagle Cycle Works
Mochdre
Newtown
Powys
SY16 4LD

Claud Butler
PO Box 3
Bridge Street
Brigg
South Humberside
DN20 8PB

Cannondale
Bike UK
40–42 Clapham High Street
London
SW4 7UR

Dawes Cycles
Wharf Road
Tyseley
Birmingham
West Midlands
B11 2EA

DBS
Jonas Oglaend
WML Sherwood Centre
Gregory Boulevard
Nottingham
NG7 6LD

Eclipse
Bike UK
40–42 Clapham High Street
London
SW4 7UR

Emmelle
Unit 3
Poulton Drive
Daleside Road Industrial Estate
Nottingham
NG2 4BN

F. W. Evans
77–79 The Cut
Waterloo
London
SE1 8LL

Falcon
see Claud Butler

Fisher
Bike UK
40–42 Clapham High Street
London
SW4 7UR

Focus Cycles
Unit 11
East Park Trading Estate
Gordon Road
Whitehall
Bristol
Avon BS5 7DH

Highpath
54 Highpath Road
Merrow
Guildford
Surrey
GU1 2QQ

High-Tech Cycles
Morgan Street
Dundee
Scotland

Holdsworth
see Claud Butler

Horizon
Two Wheels Good
35 Call Lane
Leeds
West Yorks
LS1 7BT

Hykeham (Centurion/Ermine)
Westminster Road
North Hykeham
Lincs
LN6 3QY

Bob Jackson
148 Harehills Lane
Leeds
West Yorks
LS8 5BD

Kalkhoff
The Old Vicarage
Llanellan
Abergavenny
Gwent
NP7 9HT

Kiss Miami
Cyclelogical
136–138 New Cavendish Street
London
W1M 7FG

Ron Kitching
Hookstone Park
Harrogate
North Yorks
HG2 7BZ

Laser
Bell Street Bikes
73 Bell Street
London
NW1

Marin
ATB Sales
Highfield Drive
Churchfield Industrial Estate
St Leonards
East Sussex

Marlboro
see Claud Butler

Mercian
7 Shardlow Road
Alvaston
Derbyshire
DE2 0JG

Muddy Fox
95 Manor Farm Road
Wembley
Middlesex
HA0 1BY

Orbit Cycles
Unit 8
Peartree Industrial Park
Dudley
West Midlands
DY2 0QY

Outsider
The Bicycle Chain
10 Bradbury Street
London
N16 8JN

Overbury's
138 Ashley Road
Bristol
Avon
BS6 5PA

PCM
PO Box 3
Grays
Essex
RM16 3HY

Peugeot
Cycles Peugeot (UK)
Edison Road
Bedford
MK41 0HU

Prompto
Unit 17
Metropolitan Centre
24 Derby Road
Greenford
Middx
UB6 8UG

Puch
Crown House
664–668 Dunstable Road
Luton
Beds
LU4 8SD

Raleigh
Triumph Road
Nottingham
NG7 2DD

Reflex Mountain Bike Co.
The Gate Studios
Station Road
Elstree
London
WD6 1DE

Renegade
On Your Bike
52–54 Tooley Street
London
SE1

Ridgeback
Madison Cycles
4 Horseshoe Close
London
NW2 7JJ

Chas Roberts
86 Gloucester Road
Croydon
Surrey
CR0 2DN

Saracen Cycles
PO BOX 86
Leamington Spa
Warks
CV32 6SF

Scott USA
Bert Harkins Racing
60 High Street
Berkhamstead
Herts
HP4 2BP

Shiner
Lawrence Hill
Bristol
Avon
BS5 9JB

Specialized
Caratti Sport
Unit 49, Beeches Industrial Estate
Waverley Road
Yate
Bristol
Avon
BS17 5QZ

M. Steel
2 Station Road
South Gosforth
Newcastle upon Tyne

Swallow Cycles
2 Stannetts
Laindon North Trade Centre
Essex
SS15 6DJ

Roy Swinnerton
67–71 Victoria Road
Fenton
Stoke-on-Trent
Staffs

Tushingham
The Sail Loft
Glasshouse Mill
Pateley Bridge
North Yorks
HG3 5QH

Universal Cycles
Totman Crescent
Brook Road Industrial Estate
Rayleigh
Essex
SS6 7UY

Magazines Featuring Mountain Biking

UK Publications

Bicycle Action
95 Manor Farm Road
Wembley
Middlesex
HA0 1BY

Bicycle
Cover Publications
Northern & Shell plc
PO Box 318
Mill Harbour
London
E14 9TW

Bicycle Times
Scribe Tech Ltd
Broomfield House
Belling Road
Bradford
West Yorks
BD4 7BG

BMX Action Bike
40 Bowling Green Lane
London
N1

Cycletouring
CTC
69 Meadrow
Godalming
Surrey
GU7 3HS

Cycle Trader
Turret Wheatland
177 Hagden Lane
Watford
Herts

Cycling Weekly
9–15 Ewell Road
Cheam
Surrey
SM3 8BZ

Cycling World
Stone Industrial Publications
Andrew House
2A Granville Road
Sidcup
Kent

Daily Cyclist
London Cycling Campaign
3 Stamford Street
London
SW14 7AE

Despatch Rider
PO Box 398
London
SE13 5RW

Everything Cycling
Ron Kitching
Hookstone Park
Harrogate
North Yorks

Freewheel
PO Box 740
London
NW2

Making Tracks
55 Grafton Road
New Malden
Surrey
KT3 3AA

Mountain Biking (MBC
Newsletter)
3 The Shrubbery
Albert Street
St Georges
Telford
TF2 9AS

Mountain Biking UK
Fast Trax Ltd.
Woodstock House
Luton Road
Faversham
Kent
ME13 8HQ

Winning
11 Well Lane
East Sheen
London
SW14 7AE

International Publications

Adventure Bike
22 Rue de la Concorde
1050 Brussels
Belgium

Fat Tyre Flyer
PO Box 757
Fairfax
CA 94930
USA

Irish Cycling Review
Victory Irish Promotions
82 Upper Georges Street
Dun Laoghaire
Dublin
Republic of Ireland

Mountain Bike
PO Box 989
Crested Butte
Co 81224
USA

Mountain Bike Action
PO Box 9502
Mission Hills
Ca 91345
USA

Mountain Biking
7950 Deering Ave
Canoga Park
Ca 91304
USA

Tour
Sonnenstrasse 29
Postfach 20 0101
8000 München 2
West Germany

Useful Books

Rights of Way: A Guide to Law and Practice, by Paul Clayden and John Trevelyan (published by the Ramblers' Association and Open Spaces Society, 1983).

On Your Bicycle, by James McGurn (published by John Murray, 1987).

The Bridleways of Britain, edited by Annabel Whittet (published by Whittet Books, 1986).

Out in the Country (published by the Countryside Commission, 1985; available free by sending a large SAE to their head office).

Bicycles up Kilimanjaro, by Richard and Nicholas Crane (published by the Oxford Illustrated Press, 1985).

The Ridgeway Path, by Sean Jennett (published by HMSO, 1977).

The South Downs Way, by Sean Jennett (published by HMSO, 1978).

The Pennine Way, by Tom Stephenson (published by HMSO, 1981).

Index

Page numbers in *italic* refer to the illustrations

accessories, 116–31
Allen keys, 69
aluminium frames, 21–2
angles, frames, 23–4
anti-flat preparations, 118–19
axles, 79

bags, 122–4, *123*
bars, 34, 38, 81, 120
bear trap pedals, 24
bearings: bottom brackets, 26
    lubrication, 67–8
    pedals, 24
bicycle messengers, 113–14, 118
blocks, freewheel, 27
bottom brackets, 26, 81, 82–3, *82*
brake levers, 33, *34*, 38
brakes, 11, 17–18, 31–3, *32*, *33*, 110,
    122
    checking, 85–6
    maintenance, 73–4, *73*, 79–80
    using, 39
bridleways, 56–60
British Waterways Boards, 61–2

butted tubes, 21
buying a mountain bike, 16–36

cameras, 126
cantilever brakes, 31, *32*, 122
chain breakers, 69, 94–5
chainrings, 25–6, *27*, 77–8
chains, 26, 125, *125*
    checking, 86–7
    lubrication, 66–7, *67*
    maintenance, 70–1, 78
    repairs, 94–5
chainstay protectors, 125
chrome molybdenum frames, 20–1
cleaning bikes, 64–6, *65*
clothes, 39, 89–91, 126–31, *127*,
    129, *130*
    reflective, 112–13
compasses, 95–6
competitions, 97–107
cornering, 45–7
Countryside Access Charter, 55
Crane, Nick and Dick, 13, 132, *133*
cranks, 24–5, 76, *77*, 80, 125–6

crowns, 22–3
Cyclists' Touring Club, 9, 59

dehydration, 87–8
derailleurs *see* gear mechanisms
dynamos, 112, 120

expeditions, 132–9

first aid kits, 93–4
food and drink, 87–8
footpaths, 56
footwear, 129–31
Forestry Commission, 55, 56
forks, 22–3
fox and hounds, 104–5
frames, 11, 16, *20*
  fork and crown, 22–3
  joints, 22
  maintenance, 84
  metals, 19–22
  shape, 23–4
freewheels, 27, 77–8
friction gears, 30
front wheel techniques, 47–8

gadgets, 125–6
gear levers, 33–4, 38, 80
gear mechanisms, 29–31
gears, 11, 16–18, 111
  checking, 86
  maintenance, 74–5, *74–6*, 80
  repairs, 95
  using, 39–41
gloves, 131
goggles, 90, 131
grips, 35, 120

handgrips, 35, 120
handlebars, 34, 38, 81, 120
headgear, 98, 131
headset, 81, 83, 86
hill climbs, 105

hill descents, 105
Himalayas, 134–9
HiteRite, 119–20
hub brakes, 31–3, 79–80
hub gears, 31
hubs, maintenance, 72, *72*, 79

indexed gears, 30, 34, 40, 80
injuries, 93–4
inner tubes, 29

joints, frames, 22
jumps, 50–2, *51*

lights, 112, 120
locks, 112, 124
long course racing, 100–3
lubrication, 66–8, *67*
luggage, 88–9, 122–4

McFadden, Cyra, 10
MacMillan, Kirkpatrick, 9
maintenance, 63–84
manganese molybdenum steel alloy
    frames, 21
maps, 57–9, 91
Marin County, 10
messengers, 113–14, 118
Ministry of Defence, 56
'mixte' frames, *20*, 24
Moore, John, 13
Mountain Bike Club, 14, 54, 56, 59
mudflaps, 122
mudguards, 111, 120–2, *121*

National Off-Road Bicycle
    Association (NORBA), 13, 14,
    54
National Parks, 56–7
National Trust, 56
navigation, 95–6
night riding, 112

Off-Road Code, 54–5, 56
Ordnance Survey maps, 57–8
orienteering, 104

pace-making, 92–3
panniers, 88–9, 111, 122, 123
Pearson, Ted, 13
pedals, 24, *25*
    checking, 86–7
    maintenance, 76–7, 80–1
platform pedals, 24
pumps, 118
punctures, 29, 94

racks, 122
railway lines, 60–1
Ramblers' Association, 59
reflectors, 112–13
repairs, 94–5
riding techniques, 41–52, *42, 43,
    49, 51*
rights of way, 55–60
rim brakes, 11, 31
rims, 27–8, 72, 79
road safety, 109–11
routes, 91–2
rucksacks, 88–9, 123, *123,* 124

saddles, 35, 36, 111, 119–20
    checking, 86
    covers, 119
    setting up, 37–8
safety, 95–6, 98–9, 109–11
screwdrivers, 68–9
second-hand roads, 60–2
security, 124–5
setting up bikes, 37–41
shackle locks, 112, 124
short course racing, 99–100
socks, 129
spanners, 68
speedo/milometers, 126
spoke keys, 69

spokes, 28, 71–2, *71,* 78–9
sprockets, 27
steel frames, 19–20, 21
stems, 34–5, 81
steps, 48, *49*

team events, 106–7
thumbshifters, 33–4
TIG welds, 22, 23
toolkits, 68–70, *69,* 84, 95
towpaths, 60–2
treasure hunts, 105
trespassing, 55–6, 59–60
trial events, 103–4
turning corners, 45–7
tyre levers, 69
tyres, 11, 16–18, 28–9, 110, 111,
    116–18
    anti-flat preparations, 118–19
    checking, 85–6
    competitions, 98–9
    inner tubes, 29
    maintenance, 71, 79
    valves, 29

UK Championship Final, 100
urban mountain biking, 108–15, *109*

valves, 29, 118

Walkman, 126
water bottles, 89
Wayfarer, 10
welding, joints, 22
wheel hubs, maintenance, 83–4
wheelies, 47–8
wheels, 16, 27–8
    checking, 86
    maintenance, 71–2, *71, 72,* 78–9
    quick-release, 36, 111
    repairs, 95
whistles, 95–6
wilderness races, 100–3
World Championships, 14, 101